Barbara—
Continued Success... opening
doors to opportunities.
Jama
(p.96)

SO, WHAT DO YOU DO? VOL2

SO, WHAT DO YOU DO? VOL2

Discovering the **GENIUS** *Next Door*
with One Simple Question

JOEL COMM

NEW YORK

SO, WHAT DO YOU DO? VOL2
Discovering the **GENIUS** *Next Door with One Simple Question Vol. 2*

Published in New York, New York, by Morgan James Publishing. Morgan James and The Entrepreneurial Publisher are trademarks of Morgan James, LLC. www.MorganJamesPublishing.com

The Morgan James Speakers Group can bring authors to your live event. For more information or to book an event visit The Morgan James Speakers Group at www.TheMorganJamesSpeakersGroup.com.

A free eBook edition is available with the purchase of this print book.

CLEARLY PRINT YOUR NAME ABOVE IN UPPER CASE

Instructions to claim your free eBook edition:
1. Download the BitLit app for Android or iOS
2. Write your name in **UPPER CASE** on the line
3. Use the BitLit app to submit a photo
4. Download your eBook to any device

ISBN 978-1-63047-251-1 paperback
ISBN 978-1-63047-329-7 hard cover
ISBN 978-1-63047-328-0 eBook

Cover Design by:
Rachel Lopez
www.r2cdesign.com

Interior Design by:
Bonnie Bushman
bonnie@caboodlegraphics.com

In an effort to support local communities, raise awareness and funds, Morgan James Publishing donates a percentage of all book sales for the life of each book to Habitat for Humanity Peninsula and Greater Williamsburg.

Get involved today, visit
www.MorganJamesBuilds.com

Habitat for Humanity®
Peninsula and
Greater Williamsburg
Building Partner

CONTENTS

ACKNOWLEDGEMENTS

Whenever you jump into a project involving as many moving parts as a book does, there are so many people who are essential to bringing it together. I would like to give a grateful nod to a number of those individuals who have made it happen.

To David Perdew, who now challenges our friend Ken McArthur for being the "nicest guy in Internet marketing", thank you for welcoming me into the NAMS community and for jumping on board this project. I think we've created a work that will make you and all NAMS members proud.

To Natalie Collins, my always-smiling assistant, thanks for being fabulous at communicating with all the contributors and getting everything delivered on schedule. You have earned the title "Master Cat Herder"!

To my editor, Andrea Wagner.

To David Hancock, the best publisher in the entire world, thank you for always believing in my ideas no matter how hare-brained they may be. You are a truly like a brother to me.

To my illustrious co-authors in the NAMS community, thank you for sharing your journey with me and the readers of this book. Your willingness to tell your story and share the wisdom gleaned from it will undoubtedly inspire and encourage those who read your words.

And to the many wonderful friends, both old and new, whom I have had the privilege to connect with as I emerged from my sabbatical this past year, thank you for the warm reception and friendship you have provided me. I am truly grateful to know so many amazing people that share their genius by doing what you do every day.

Finally, to Zach and Jenna, as your father it is my greatest joy and privilege to see you enter adulthood with such firm foundations and strong character. I know you already bless those who you encounter, and I can't wait to watch your impact grow as you share your God-given genius with the world around you. Regardless of what else I achieve in my life, you two will always be my greatest accomplishments!

INTRODUCTION

By Joel Comm

It was shortly after I began compiling inspirational stories for the first edition of So, What Do You Do? that a name was shared with me by several associates. The name was David Perdew. Those who told me I needed to meet David were incredulous that I had not heard of David, nor his exceptional business-building community, NAMS. I soon discovered that NAMS was an acronym for Novice-to-Advanced Marketing System.

After meeting David myself, I was incredulous with myself that I had not met him previously and that I was just becoming acquainted with the work being accomplished through his community. I knew I had to discover more about NAMS for myself.

It was early February 2014 that I was invited to speak at NAMS' annual conference and finally had the opportunity to meet David Perdew, his charming wife Charlsa, and members of the NAMS community. What I discovered left me inspired and with a desire to become part of NAMS.

David and his team have succeeded in creating a diverse community of entrepreneurs who are givers in every sense of the word. While each determined to succeed in their respective niches, there's a sense of family that is a rarity in the online business world. If a rising tide does indeed lift all boats, the extraordinary people who are part of the NAMS community are all on the rise.

It's with great pride that I am pleased to present you with the second volume of So, What Do You Do: Discovering the Genius Next Door with One Simple Question, comprised entirely of inspirational and entrepreneurial stories from the NAMS community.

Whether you devour the book in one reading or if you savor stories one day at a time, you are sure to connect with the hearts and minds of the people within. With as many unique experiences as there are contributors, I know that these stories will encourage you on your journey, cause you to see the world in different ways and provide you with valuable tips and strategies applicable to your life and business.

While there are geniuses all up and down the street where you live (and at least one at your own address!), it's my hope that the NAMS community of geniuses will inspire and equip you to keep moving forward as you seek to bring value to the world around you.

Do good stuff!

—Joel Comm
New York Times Best-Selling Author,
International Speaker, Serial Entrepreneur

LEGACY OF SUCCESS

By David Perdew

'm getting older now. Even though I still feel young, I know that the Social Security disbursements aren't far off. As we age, we older folks begin to think, What has my life meant? What kind of legacy will I leave?

When that word—legacy—comes up, most folks have grandiose ideas. They think about a hospital wing or a scholarship in their name. They might think about the display at the local library announcing their hefty donation. Those legacies are great, but I've learned that the impact I have on the world is much more important.

When I was younger I wanted respect. I wanted to be somebody, like the successful, independent, self-made businessmen who surrounded me. They could walk into a restaurant in my hometown and greet everyone with a handshake and a smile. Those men seemed important. They were not just big fish in a small pond but men who had made an impact on other people's lives. I wanted to be like them, to be greeted as important and successful everywhere I went. Like most young people, though, all I noticed were the trappings of success instead of the hard work that predicates it.

I tried to don an attitude of success without doing the real work, but for an undisciplined, self-centered fool like me, no good would come of it. This skewed worldview eventually revealed itself. For example, I always said I wanted to write great fiction. Truthfully, though, I wanted my romanticized notion of a famous writer's life. Waking at 5 am to write required more discipline than I possessed.

To pursue success before laying the foundation that makes it worthwhile is like holding jello in your hands: sooner or later it slips away. Heck, the only signs of success I recognized were:

- Money, which equaled success, so I wanted lots of it;
- Power, which meant you could boss around the people who worked for you;
- Power and Money together, so others deferred to your requests and seemed to admire you;
- Respect (or even being feared), so you could feel superior.

Reading that list now makes me a little embarrassed, like I was a horrendous person. I'm not proud of that. Nobody's to blame for those very ugly ideas, though I tried to blame a lot of people for many years. My family, including my kids, paid the price for my immaturity.

Truthfully, I didn't know any better, and it took years for me to learn a different way of living. But eventually I did learn, by the guidance of my father's voice echoing in my head.

All my life, Dad voiced his clichés, haunting me with seemingly unattainable goals. Eventually, though, those clichés began to make sense. (I know. It's always a shock when our parents are suddenly wise.) Even as I realized the value of Dad's platitudes, I also learned that I needed to amend them for my life.

Here are a few of the most meaningful to me.

"There's no better way to kill time than to work it to death."

Though no one ever told me I was lazy, I saw myself that way compared to Dad. He was always working on a project or building something; in comparison, I was a real slacker.

So I became obsessed with work. A life without work, paid or not, is a life without contribution. It's a huge part of my life because I love to solve problems. I realize now that my dad was also a great problem solver.

On the other hand, work is not everything. It's not happiness. Thus, my amended version of Dad's saying is, "There's no better way to solve problems than to work them to death."

Another one of my father's favorite sayings was, "Don't confuse me with the facts."

This sentiment used to make me so angry. It was just stupid, I thought. It is impossible to have a discussion with someone who is blind to the facts; open-mindedness and a willingness to debate facts are essential. But I made sure to arm myself with indisputable facts before discussing anything. My goal was always to have the answer and to be right, even when I wasn't.

Now, when I contemplate that phrase, I understand it refers to conviction, dedication, and belief. Arguments can enlighten, and opinions can change, but facts can also be manipulated to support one's point of view. Over the years, I've observed how manipulation of facts can destroy people's lives and souls. I now search myself for my core beliefs and hold on to them for dear life. Without those convictions, I am an empty man. I must stay true to myself even when the world is falling apart around me.

My new variation of Dad's old saying is, "You CAN'T confuse me with the facts; I'm driven by my core beliefs."

The last of Dad's sayings goes, "When poverty comes through the door, love goes out the window."

At a young age, this thought was especially damning. I wondered how a guy like me, who lived paycheck to paycheck for so many years, could possibly maintain a relationship. I decided I had to seem rich, one way or another. For me, this meant hiding my financial woes from my wife. When the checkbook balance hovered near zero, I feared being honest with her because I thought she would fly out the window. Unfortunately, by concealing the burdens of life and my fears from my children's mother, I made all the decisions for her—and then resented her for it. So away she flew anyway.

I modified Dad's saying to this: "When trust goes out the door, so does love."

So many times, my Dad was right, but I did not truly hear the meaning and wisdom behind his words. My perception was wrong then; it was all about me.

Now, instead, I think about who I am and what I'm leaving behind. Not what I will leave when I die, but rather what I'll leave each time I have a conversation, or work with a colleague, or introduce friends.

When I meet people for the first time, I wonder, Are you better for having met me? Am I serving you in ways that enrich your life?

People who met and worked with my eighty-five-year old father decades ago continue to tell him how much he meant in their lives. Now that's a legacy. Rather than your name on one building, your memory is imprinted on hundreds of hearts.

A prayer attributed to St. Francis describes the personal change I experienced over my life and the legacy I wish to leave:

> *O Divine Master, Grant that I may not so much seek*
> *To be consoled as to console;*
> *To be understood as to understand;*
> *To be loved as to love.*
> *For it is in giving that we receive;*
> *It is in pardoning that we are pardoned;*
> *And it is in dying that we are born to eternal life.*
> *And I would have amended that prayer with another line:*
> *"To be respected and honored as to respect and honor others."*

ABOUT THE AUTHOR

 As the CEO and chief architect of NAMS (the Novice to Advanced Marketing System), David Perdew has used all his skills as a journalist, consultant and entrepreneur to build one of the most successful and fastest growing business training workshops available today at NextNAMS.com and it's supporting membership site at NAMSInsiders.com.

The Novice to Advanced Marketing System is a step-by-step training system focusing on Team, Training Tools to help novice to advanced business people become even more successful.

He took a year off in 2003 to personally build a 2200 square foot log cabin in north Alabama where he and his wife and two dogs and a cat live on 95 acres of forest with four streams and a 60-foot waterfall.

Connect with David and find out more about NAMS at:

www.facebook.com/NicheAffiliateMarketingSystem

twitter.com/mynamsystem

www.linkedin.com/in/drperdew

THE PROBLEM WITH "SOMETHING TO FALL BACK ON"

By Geoff Hoff

'Ve always been a creative sort. I spent my childhood making up stories and acting them out, painting and drawing and even singing (though not well, I'm told). I wrote my first full short story when I was nine. My mother encouraged this. She even entertained us by drawing amazing, swirling pictures with oil pastel crayons.

As I got older, though, and it appeared I might choose an artistic endeavor for a life path, she began hinting that I might want to find "something to fall back on." When I announced that I wanted to study acting in college, she said that was great, but to make sure I also studied something I could actually make money at or I'd be broke and unhappy all my life. Guidance counselors and teachers also hinted that creativity wasn't very practical for an adult. And by "hinted," I mean they said so outright.

I resisted it, of course. I graduated from college with a Bachelor of Arts degree in Theatre. (Yes, I spell it with an <u>re</u>. I have no problem admitting to being pretentious. I like to think it's part of my charm.) My plan after college was to spend a year in northern California with my brother and his wife while acclimating to life after school. Then I would move to San Francisco and disappear into a repertory company and spend my days happily ensconced in a life in theatre. However, as Robert Burns said to the wee mouse, "The best-laid schemes o' mice an' men/Gang aft agley." Okay, so my schemes weren't all that well laid out to begin with, but they did gang a bit agley.

I got to the little town in northern California and found a job at a pizza parlor. The town had only one movie house, and it mostly showed movies that oozed too much testosterone for my taste. The nearest alternative was in Sacramento, a 45-minute drive down the highway. If I wanted to see something that didn't have Sylvester Stallone in it, I would need to find someone else who wanted to go and who also had a car.

One afternoon I decided I needed to see a movie, but no one I knew wanted to go. My friend Vern, however, who lived right across the street from me, offered the use of his car. I decided on The China Syndrome, which was playing at one of the bigger movie complexes in the outskirts of Sacramento, gathered Vern's keys, and journeyed hence.

The movie, starring Jane Fonda, Michael Douglas, Jack Lemmon, and Wilford Brimley, was a political thriller very loosely based on the Three Mile Island incident. A young, naive reporter (Fonda) accidentally stumbles upon evidence that the safety inspections for the building of the local nuclear plant were fudged, and those responsible ranged from the halls of corporations to the government. The script was tight, the direction flawless. The tension built slowly but steadily to a fever pitch. Jack Lemmon, an actor I had always admired, was never better. I was moved. Stunned might be a better word. On the ride home in that borrowed car, I decided I wanted to be part of an industry that could produce something so powerful. The next day I put in my notice at the pizza parlor.

A month later, I was living in a squalid little room in Hollywood, scared but happy to be on the new journey. Then life took over. I got a job, which led to another job. Then another. Then, contrary to all expectations, I learned a bit about computers and became the computer guy at a law firm, which led to an entirely new career. I acted in a few plays, directed a play or two, and taught an acting class for a couple of years, but I never quite broke through. I eventually gave it up and concentrated more on my new career in tech. I had "fallen back" on something.

The creative spirit went to sleep a bit. It didn't die completely, though. It itched at the edges of my life, so I still wrote—short stories, novels, and poetry. No one ever saw them, of course; it was all just so I would not fade into a stifled death. I read anything I could get my hands on and saw every movie I could. I visited museums and saw plays. That really wasn't enough, though; the itch was getting intense, so I started studying the process of creativity, first within myself, then looking at how other people expressed, suppressed, encouraged, or experienced their creative pursuits.

As I studied, I was surprised to discover that creativity wasn't this mysterious thing that only a few people were gifted with. It was available to anyone and it could be taught in very practical ways. I decided to test that assumption and taught a short story writing class online that was quite successful. Everyone in the class finished with a decent short story, even though many of the participants started out thinking it would be impossible!

I expanded the concept and started teaching business people how to access their own native creativity and use it in their business: as a problem solving tool, to create and market products, and even the mundane stuff like writing blog posts and sales pages. I still do some tech work, but concentrate much more on my own creative pursuits and teaching others to pursue theirs.

So what does this mean for you? Good question.

You are creative. I believe everyone is. Look at any child if you don't believe me. Children appear on the scene ready to play, to create worlds of wonder for themselves. They're wired for it. If you still feel you aren't, it's just that someone, somewhere along the way convinced you otherwise. Whoever that was should be slapped. Yes, even if they had your best interests at heart, even if it was you who did the convincing because you wanted to be practical. I can prove to you in about 20 seconds that you're creative. Don't believe me? Try this:

1. Sit down and think of a lemon. The skin is yellow, almost waxy smooth. It has a slightly bumpy texture when you run your finger across it.
2. Now imagine picking up a sharp knife and cutting into that lemon. At first, the knife resists a little, then slices through easily. When you open the lemon, the inside is cool and moist. It emits a pleasant odor. Imagine that odor for a moment. It's tart and clean-smelling.
3. Touch the inside with the tip of your finger. It's wet, but it's a smooth wetness. You can also feel the lemon pulp.
4. Now pick up one half of the lemon and raise it up to your mouth. Squeeze just one small drop of the juice and let it drip onto your tongue. That cool, tart drop rolls to the back of your tongue. Let it sit there for a moment.

Did you pucker? Did your mouth water, even a little?

Congratulations! You are officially creative! You took an imaginary lemon and visualized it. You touched it. You actually tasted it, and it made your mouth water. But there isn't a lemon in sight, so what made your mouth water? Where is the lemon?

You created that lemon out of nothing, out of your imagination. You created something out of nothing, and that something had a physical effect on you. You are creative.

Once you know you're creative, it's just a matter of finding ways to develop it so you are in charge and don't have to wait for the muse to inspire you. (The muse is really you, after all, and you can inspire yourself whenever you want to, once you learn how!)

Now go forth and create!

ABOUT THE AUTHOR

Geoff Hoff is a best-selling author and has been an actor, acting teacher, standup comic and popular blogger. He studies and writes about the process of creativity and of marketing, and teaches creative writing and marketing courses on the Internet. He is co-owner with Connie Ragen Green of Hunter's Moon Publishing.

Geoff grew up in a small town in Northern New Jersey that no longer exists, graduated from a small college in Spokane, Washington that no longer exists and has learned to distrust permanence. He has been called "gently subversive" by a fan, a description he finds apt.

You can read more at his writing blog: TipsOnWriting.net/blog/, on his tech blog: GeoffHoff.com or his personal humor blog: ThatWouldBeMe.net

Connect with Geoff at:

www.facebook.com/geoff.hoff/

twitter.com/geoffhoff

www.linkedin.com/in/geoffhoffonline/

THE BEST SHIPS ARE THE FRIENDSHIPS!

By Captain Lou Edwards

Imagine living your dream lifestyle, getting paid to explore distant shores. Cruising the world for free, with your own highly-profitable group events at sea, while earning thousands of dollars for yourself, your company, or your charity. You are meeting the most interesting people and helping change lives!

This is my life now, but it wasn't always like this for me. I was an only child born to poor, struggling parents in Brooklyn, aged 62 and 42. I was orphaned as a teenager when my parents both passed away within a few years of each other.

Needing to find a way to survive, I dropped out of junior high to join the circus. Well, it felt like a circus, being on the road with people whose names were Andre The Giant, Classy Freddie Blassie, 601-pound Haystacks Calhoun, 'Polish Power' Ivan Putski, and 'Manager Of Champions,' Captain Lou Albano. He was the original Captain Lou; may he rest in peace.

It was 1978, before pro wrestling became a billion-dollar sports entertainment empire under Vince McMahon and Hulk Hogan. By forming a few key friendships, I was taken in by this colorful crowd and quickly became the voice of a New York-based wrestling talk radio show, as well as ring announcer, interviewer, and color commentator.

The wrestling community was a lifeline for me at a terrifyingly lonely time. They kept me off the streets and got me to overcome my shyness. These became the most fun four years of my life—until now.

In 1982, well-meaning friends and my few remaining relatives strongly suggested that wrestling would never be big and that I should focus on getting a "real" job, so I quit. Big mistake. Never take advice from people whose lives you wouldn't want! I have no regrets, though. This first phase of my life taught me showmanship. The next one would teach me salesmanship and survival!

One day at the racetrack, I befriended a lovely man—actually a degenerate gambler I'll call "Norman"—by simply asking him, "So What Do You Do?" That question led me to my next crazy career selling plastic furniture covers to poor people in the projects in each of the five boroughs. My time with "Norman" and his partners "No-Neck" and "Melon-Head" led me to a clientele of drug dealers, crackheads, mobsters, corrupt politicians, and welfare cheats. That was just business as usual for the inner city in the '80s and '90s.

They all wanted sweaty plastic slipcovers to protect (and destroy the look) of their nice new furniture. Suffice it to say, I went from one kind of circus to another, getting a very different education along the way. I was just happy to stay alive and make an honest living.

After paying my dues for several years, I graduated to "Blind Man," selling custom window treatments and upholstery in better neighborhoods and to a more diverse clientele. The joke on the street was that I became New York's only heterosexual interior decorator. Of course I delighted at the hundreds of women who invited me into their bedrooms…to measure their windows!

The money was good, but after a while I started feeling like a glorified taxi driver, spending more time fighting traffic in the five boroughs of

NYC than actually making sales. And quibbling over color swatches and our "fifty shades of beige and mauve" became less and less fulfilling. (Grey wasn't big yet).

After twenty years of making a living, I decided to start making a life! I dreamed of world travel, helping fulfill people's dreams and fantasies, and making a difference in their lives as well as my own.

Like many others who have never been on a modern-day cruise ship, I used to think cruises were just for the newlywed or the nearly dead, and that the average age of the guests was deceased! Then, a friend talked me into going with her on something called The Big Red Boat. I was instantly hooked on cruising. I knew I had to persevere if I were to realize my dream lifestyle visiting exotic beaches and distant shores.

Woody Allen said, "Eighty percent of success is showing up." In January 2003 I took his advice and attended my very first Internet marketing conference called "The BIG Seminar" in Dallas, Texas.

I hoped to learn how to put my new "Little Shop Of Cruises" travel agency online and reach out to a greater audience via the web. At that point, it was part hobby, part dream, as I was still a Blind Man (in the window treatment industry).

Never did I imagine the people I would meet and the friendships I would make in Dallas that weekend. It would profoundly change my business model and the course of my life! Another attendee asked if I could arrange a similar event on a cruise ship, sort of a "seminar-at-sea" combined with a fun vacation vibe. She asked if we could do mastermind meetings and JVs in a giant hot tub, sipping piña coladas, and sailing away from sun-drenched islands in the Bahamas or Caribbean.

Not even realizing that JV stood for "joint venture," I instantly said, "Sure, we can do this. In fact, that's my specialty!" It wasn't actually my specialty yet, but I figured "fake it 'til you make it," right?

Until that point, I had made all the wrong investments. My special stock market strategy was to buy high and sell when my stock hit zero. I should have known not to trust a financial advisor named Marcus Finagle. I bought my first property, a waterfront condo with views of the NYC skyline, at the very top, right before the real estate tumble. This time, I knew I needed to invest in my one best shot at a bigger ROI—me!

At that event in Dallas, I bought all the info products and software packages and discovered how to automate the booking process online, how to stop selling one-on-one in person or by phone, and start selling one-on-many through websites, webinars, live stage presentations, and more.

On Halloween weekend of 2003, my first "special-event-at-sea" debuted with about 50 students and speakers. We did just about everything wrong, but it was a huge success. It was that "Affiliate Marketers Cruise" that led me to transform my new business model from one of a million travel agencies to one-in-a-million producer of specially-themed niche group vacations.

Branding myself "Captain Lou" the cruise guru worked well, and I quickly became the go-to guy for people who wanted to wow their audiences with an unforgettable, profitable, and life-changing experience. I started producing "Special-Events-At-Sea" for casino chip collectors, opera groups, multi-generational family reunions, real estate trainers, marketing coaches, consultants, and gurus.

I later developed a Marketers Cruise, a true peer-to-peer networking and mastermind vacation that would draw the world's top marketers for an adventure of a lifetime. The Marketers Cruise would give back to the Internet marketing community that had done so much for our businesses. Top marketers from 17 countries around the world put everything on hold to join our cruise family each year, including David Perdew, creator of the NAMS community, and many bootstrap entrepreneurs who have contributed chapters here about their personal voyages and passions.

The Marketers Cruise is my flagship product. It's what turned "Captain WHO?" into "Captain Lou."

This event, where profitable deals are made while having fun on vacation, has been the springboard for my other life-changing "group events at sea," such as an annual Murder Mystery Cruise, an eBay cruise, a United States Marine Corp Veterans Cruise, and a Legacy Cruise about what we leave behind by learning to pay it forward.

I now help develop niche groups for entrepreneurs who want to bring their own audiences on the Marketers Cruise or any cruise ship adventure in the Caribbean, Alaska, Hawaii, or Europe, instead of some stuffy hotel conference room.

It's hard to imagine that an eighth grade dropout who has never seen the inside of a high school has gone on to lecture at colleges and speak on stages around the world.

It's taken me 35 years to become an overnight success, but that's all right. We didn't have the Internet back then or access to visionaries like Joel Comm, David Perdew, and all the inspiring geniuses-next-door who are featured in this book. Now your dreams and fantasies can be fulfilled much faster.

I'm finally living my dream, getting paid to travel the world, living the laptop lifestyle and encouraging you to do the same. Perhaps you'll consider joining me on one of my upcoming group cruise events, so you can discover the rest of the story.

Remember, it doesn't matter what SHIP you're sailing on or what journey gets you to your destination as long as you are with friends. After all, the best ships are the FRIENDships. See you on the Lido deck!

ABOUT THE AUTHOR

When not speaking at industry events or teaching his "Million-Dollar Groups System" to other travel professionals, Captain Lou prides himself on showing leaders like you how to cruise the world for free with your own highly profitable groups at sea. For more information, please visit: SpecialEventsAtSea.com.

He is the author of a book on group cruises: ThinkGroupsAndGrowRich.com (for travel agents only) and a CD on How To Cruise The World For FREE: JustAddWater.CaptainLou.com (for group leaders).

Lou is also the producer/planner of the amazing annual mastermind and networking vacation known as The Marketers Cruise.

For more information, and to join us, please RSVP at: NAMSCruise.com

The FRIENDships start here:
facebook.com/captainlouedwards
linkedin.com/in/captainlou
twitter.com/captainlou
youtube.com/captainlou

PROSPER BY DESIGN

By Melissa Galt

A rmed with a degree in hospitality management from Cornell University, I dove into hotel purchasing with both feet. I moved cities, states, and companies every eight months for five years, climbing the ladder of success and making good money, while being one of the few females in the field.

If you ate it, drank it, wrote with it, or slept on it, I bought it. From the Hilton in Ryetown, New York, to the Grand Hotel on Mackinac Island, Michigan, from Opryland Hotel in Nashville, Tennessee, to Calloway Gardens in Columbus, Georgia, I was the turn-around artist. They hired me to organize and install systems in purchasing departments, taking them from bleeding red to squarely in the black.

I was really good at what I did, but unfortunately, I was also miserable. (Does that sound familiar?) My favorite part of every new position was space-planning my storerooms and installing the systems. The day-to-day operations bored me silly; it was time for a change. I quit.

My mother had passed away very suddenly just five years earlier when I was 24. I was finally coming to the big takeaway from her death. Life is too perishable, too short, and entirely too unpredictable

17

to spend it doing something you don't love, no matter how good at it you may be.

Having one degree already, I wanted a fast path to a new career loaded with creativity. I had originally wanted to pursue costume design in the footsteps of my godmother, Edith Head. She holds the record for her eight Oscar wins in costume design, for movies including *The Sting*, *Dead Men Don't Wear Plaid*, and Hitchcock's *Rear Window*.

I had gotten into one of the best schools in the country for costume design, but I didn't have the confidence to follow my dream. I was certain that the only reason I'd gotten in was Edith's recommendation instead of my own merit. Lack of confidence killed that dream, so I chose another in the creative realm.

I'd been designing my own interiors since my college apartment and helped friends with theirs. Interior design beckoned, and I enrolled in a three-year program in Birmingham, Alabama, that I could finish in two years with credits transferred.

My creative journey was firmly underway. It didn't hurt that my great-grandfather, America's most famous (though not favorite) architect, Frank Lloyd Wright, showed up in all of my textbooks. (I didn't realize he was such a big deal until I went to design school. I guess design is the genes.)

I picked up a full-time job in design while attending full-time classes; I was on fire. For every project assigned in school, I turned in four. My classmates were jealous because they could barely finish one. My instructors refused to grade more than one project, so I let my classmates vote on which one I would submit. I still got straight A's. When you are on passion with purpose, you are unstoppable! I graduated in two years as planned and started looking for a bigger pond to play in. Atlanta was next.

I had changed design jobs every eighteen months for three years. It was an improvement over every eight months in hotels, but just barely. The writing was on the wall: I had to create my own opportunity and jump into the wild blue yonder of owning my own business.

The timing caught me off guard. I was $70K in debt, living in a cramped apartment with too many credit card bills and a big car payment. I had to scramble. I landed on my feet thanks to my hotel experience, with a job supervising a catering kitchen weekends and teaching decorating classes at Evening at Emory on weeknights. It left me days to work with clients. It was a rocky start, but it was a start.

At a year and a half referrals kicked in and the business doubled every year for the first five years. It then slowed to a comfortable 20% growth. While I continued teaching at Emory because it proved to be great marketing (my clients were busy professionals, after all), the income went from being living income to supporting my annual travels, an awesome transition.

At the five-year mark I started to connect with colleagues and found that my results were rather extraordinary. In fact, my revenues were five times more than most independent designers (and it wasn't my talent but my marketing.)

They started asking me how I'd done it. How did I market my business so effectively? How did I regularly get clients to invest so much more in their projects? How did I create a close ratio of 90%? How did I create lifetime client loyalty? How had I gotten off that painful revenue rollercoaster of lots of business then no business?

I realized there were two keys to my success. The first was that I was in love with my work and I had effectively designed my business to support the life I wanted to live and the lifestyle that I wanted. (Believe me, I didn't start out that way. I came to that decision when I found my business was consuming my life, and I realized I had to redesign it.) Travel is a hobby and my design business afforded me the chance to visit India, Nepal, Greece, China, Africa, Australia, New Zealand, Bali and many more awesome locations.

The second key was that I never sold my clients. Marketing, for me, was (and still is) about being magnetic and enthusiastic about my chosen path and being genuine in my desire to solve my clients' problems. It wasn't about putting on a veneer. Every business owner struggles with selling, but the answer is to tap into the magnetism and educate on the value you provide, the problems you can solve, and the difference you make.

When I began teaching my colleagues, the first step was to find out what they wanted the whole of their life to look like so that we could design their business to deliver that.

The second step was to reignite their passion so they were genuinely tuned in, turned on, engaged, and connected to their work in a way that attracted clients magnetically. I like to call this 'being the star you are.' I got that from my mom.

Growing up with an Academy Award winner in the house was always a bit dramatic. My mom, the late actress Anne Baxter, knew at seven years old that she wanted to act. She built her life around that dream and focused on growing her talent at every chance. (You may remember her as the young Egyptian princess in *The Ten Commandments*, the one who is in love with Moses but has to marry Ramses.)

I looked at my mother's passion and my great-grandfather's famous focus on architecture and how it impacted the people living in his homes. I also looked at my godmother's successful rise in a profession she knew nothing about when she started in her late thirties. I realized it matters far less what you pursue than that you pursue it with absolute focus, drive, and passion.

Once your big vision is in place, you can design your business to serve and support it. I took what great-grandfather did with homes and lifestyle and transitioned from designing environments to designing business and life success.

Working with designers, I realized that they are service-based professionals engaged in providing transformation of a client's environment. The proven strategies I use also work outrageously well for coaches and consultants, who transform their client's health and well-being, or their client's business, or their client's life, or their client's relationships, or their client's finances. What I fast discovered is that my

Systems background gave me a big leg up with bright shiny opportunity chasers (aren't we all?). By implementing solid systems, we remove the overwhelming chaos and reclaim wasted time.

Today, I am privileged to work with my clients to clearly define what they want their life to look like, feel like, sound like, smell like, and taste like at the very start of working together. It's vital to know the whole picture so the business is designed to serve and support your whole life.

We also zero in on the ideal client profile. I allow only three clients, because when I began in design I said "yes" to everyone who showed up. While I made good money, I had no time to enjoy it. When I started to be selective and work exclusively with my ideal clients, my income doubled even though the time I spent in my business dramatically decreased, allowing me more time for fun, friends, family, and travel. When you work with only your ideal clients and stop leaving money and opportunity on the table, you'll find you can work with far fewer clients, make far more money, and enjoy it infinitely more.

Business isn't easy; it is fun and wildly rewarding when you are actively engaged in your pursuit of passion with purpose. The impact you can have is limited only by your vision and your reach. I love expanding my clients' visions and enhancing their reach to create a globally positive difference.

Success doesn't happen by default; it happens by design. You need a carefully crafted custom blueprint that takes into account your unique gifts, education, experience, expertise, and personality. They are the gold you must mine to become magnetic and unstoppable.

I'm here to guide you into who you want to be, direct you into what you need to do, and coach you on the how of designing your business for your best life now!

ABOUT THE AUTHOR

Identified by Forbes as one of the Top 20 Women of Influence for Entrepreneurs to follow, Melissa Galt is the female entrepreneur's success coach. In the last decade, she has worked with thousands of female business owners to blueprint outrageous business success and design awesome lives. Melissa takes you from out of focus and overwhelm to clarity of purpose, on path with passion, profiting with your talent, and living the life of your dreams. Prospering by Design is her mission to show you how to turn your work into purpose and your purpose into a global positive impact. Melissa is the author of Celebrate Your Life! and 7 Surefire Steps to Marketing that Make You Money.

To find out more about Melissa visit melissagalt.com

Connect with Melissa at:

facebook.com/prosperingbydesign

twitter.com/melissagalt

linkedin.com/in/melissagalt

google.com/+MelissaGaltONLY

THE "I CAN"

By Peggy McAloon

M y body floated upward through the black void toward the light. I struggled to determine where I was in the black liquid that enveloped my body.

Pain! A pain more intense than anything I had ever experienced. I tried to fight the ascent but continued to move toward the intense pulsating light beyond my eyelids. I struggled to escape, but there was no control over my body. I floated closer to the white light, and my head nearly exploded in agony.

Voices! Who were the people talking? They spoke about a body in the fetal position and the need to tie arms and legs down. I heard them call each other by name.

I floated higher, and the light became even more brilliant. The light blasted through my closed eyelids and exploded deep inside my head. The intensity of the pain reached a climax beyond my comprehension. I tried to scream at the voices to turn the light off, but my mouth wouldn't respond. I looked down at the fathomless black hole below me and dove quickly back down to that place where I was safe only minutes ago. The horror ended.

This is what I remember of the time I was in a coma. I floated toward the light many times, but the pain forced me back into the depths of minimal human existence. When the brain swells as a result of an injury, the body responds by providing a protective, cocoon-like environment. Life is put on hold as the healing begins and swelling subsides; otherwise you would go insane from the pain.

My husband and I had taken our little boys on an outing and were heading home when the truck crossed the center line. I have heard people discuss situations like this as "happening in slow motion," and that was my perception. I sat in the passenger seat and watched the truck move directly toward us. I twisted around in the seat, pushing my sons' faces into the backseat cushions. In the 1970s there were no safety seats for toddlers. In that slow-motion moment, I visualized them flying through the windshield.

My body twisted on impact, and my head smashed into the windshield. In the emergency room, they placed a collar on me and told me I had whiplash. That was all. One week later I collapsed. I had developed meningitis of the brain lining. The doctors speculated that a virus had entered through the fracture in my skull. The deep coma that resulted kept me hospitalized for several weeks. I was finally released to return home but not to a normal life. Days turned into weeks and months as I struggled with constant migraines and difficulty with movement. I couldn't tolerate more than two or three hours of activity a day.

I was the sales manager of a Century 21 real estate office in Minnesota when the accident occurred. My husband and I were in the process of purchasing the business. In a heartbeat I went from being an award-winning realtor earning a medium five-figure salary to an invalid. I was unable to take care of my children or myself.

The sudden loss of income and mounting medical bills depleted our bank account quickly. We were forced to use credit cards to purchase groceries. The financial stress only intensified my inability to function. We were forced to tap the equity in our home.

The words from my mouth were upside down and backward, even though I heard them correctly in my head. My husband became so frustrated that he began to play a game with the children. He encouraged them to talk backwards, too. I was humiliated at being made fun of in front of the boys. Yellow sticky notes appeared all over the house to remind me to feed the kids, wash the dishes, and most embarrassing, go to the bathroom. My children could read, and inside that part of my brain that still functioned, I worried about what they must think of me.

Life didn't improve much over the next couple years. The doctors decided to send me to Sister Kinney Institute in Minneapolis, where I would participate in the Pain Center program to "learn to live like this." Those were the words the doctor used that day.

I cried all the way home. All I knew for sure was that I didn't ever want to learn to live like this. My children needed a mother, and I was unable to function. My husband needed a partner, and I was missing.

The damage done to the right frontal lobe of my brain created problems with left body function. There were days when I couldn't use my left arm. I had problems controlling my left leg, too. Drugs further complicated my life. Every specialist I saw prescribed narcotics to diminish the debilitating pain, and they paralyzed what little functionality I still possessed.

After my family doctor confirmed I would go to the Pain Center, all I could think about was dying. I had been that low once before in my life. After years of unspeakable abuse as a child, I tried to commit suicide at 16. This day was no different. If I were gone, my husband could remarry, and my children would have a mother who could take care of them.

I collapsed in a chair and the tears wouldn't stop. I remembered the doctors so many years ago when they told my mother it was too late to pump my stomach. It would be several hours before they'd know whether I would live or die. When I heard that, I suddenly wanted to live more than anything. I begged God to let me live.

He had answered my prayers that day thirteen years earlier. Was I really willing to give up again? I called a friend instead of reaching for the pills. Her husband had died recently, and she was probably the only person I knew who had lost as much as I had. We talked, we cried, and we tried to just make it through the day.

The next morning I woke up angry. It was a fury unlike anything I had ever experienced. God had brought me to my knees the day before, but now I was willing to let him guide me.

After the boys headed to school, I was drawn to a closet where I had stored boxes from my childhood home. Those boxes had been there for years, and I hadn't bothered to look inside them. I had no idea what I was searching for. I had more energy than I had experienced since the accident. As I dug through the second box, my hand felt a cold, round object. I pulled it out of the box and held it high.

In my hand was an old metal vegetable can containing pencils and a ruler. I made it when I was five with the help of my grandfather. I had been a prisoner in my own home for months as a result of rheumatic fever, and he found me crying at the window as I watched all the other kids playing at the school across the street. I was sobbing that I couldn't do anything. Grandpa led me into the kitchen, found the old can and some additional supplies, and guided me through the project. When we were finished he held up the decorated can and asked, "What do you think this is?"

"I don't know, Grandpa," I laughed. His joy and excitement were catching. His kind heart could make even the most damaged child smile.

"This is an I Can!" he explained lovingly. "Look closely at what we cut out. It is the letter I in all different colors, shapes, and sizes. I don't ever want to hear you say you can't do something again. You can do anything in this life that you want to. You just have to believe in yourself, your talents, and your strengths."

It was one of the most important gifts an adult could ever give to a child—the gift of unwavering faith in oneself.

It wasn't an easy journey, but over the next five years, I embraced the message of the I Can and regained most of my abilities. I played with an electronic memory game called Simon for hours each day. That helped me reprogram my brain. I demanded that the doctors give me exercise, diet, meditation. I made the rules.

My marriage didn't survive the frustrations of my inabilities, but I did thrive again. I entered a new field that provided set hours each day rather than the sporadic hours of real estate. I had a long and extremely lucrative career until I retired a couple of years ago. The boys grew to adulthood and are the most amazing people. I am a loving wife, mother, and grandmother, and I am living my dream in retirement, writing a fantasy series about a little girl who is recruited by winged creatures from another dimension to help them protect the children of Earth. Through my protagonist's adventures, I hope to encourage children who are being hurt to find the courage to seek help and motivate other young readers to help people who are in trouble. My goal is to inspire children to reach their highest potential and to protect themselves from the dangers that exist in this challenging world.

We all face obstacles in life. There are days that I wonder how I managed to survive everything. The answer lies somewhere between believing in myself and having the courage to face the challenges I encountered on my journey. The message I share with you and children everywhere is to never give up. Faith and perseverance will lead you through. I would not have believed in 1978 that I could write a book, but that was my childhood dream and I refused to give it up. What was your dream?

The I Can sits in a prominent place in my home. It signifies the best that humanity can offer in hope to any child. My grandfather gave me the faith to believe in myself. My God had never forsaken me. I had simply given up on myself for far too long. My prayers were answered when I was humble enough to listen to the answers. I was finally able to see beyond myself and understand that my sons were my finest achievement in life and that their future was worth fighting a nearly impossible battle for.

What would this world become if every child made their very own I Can with a loving adult who helped them to believe their dreams can become their reality?

ABOUT THE AUTHOR

Peggy McAloon, CBF, retired from a career in sales and commercial credit in 2010. As the national sales manager, she led workshops and seminars, contributed to various publications and newspapers, and published her first book, *The Art of Business Credit Investigation*, in the days when business data was beginning to become available online. She is also a recognized watercolor artist who has received national awards for her efforts in the conservation of water resources.

Peggy's journey through child abuse, depression, and a debilitating car accident elevated her desire to help children cope with their challenges. To that end, she has created a fantasy series for youth that deals with the very real issues they face. Her first novel, *Elle Burton and the Reflective Portals*, was released in May, 2014.

You can learn more about Peggy's thoughts on the thornier issues of parenting at www.peggymcaloon.com. You can visit her author page at on.fb.me/1ozeJAG and her parental resource page at on.fb.me/1mK8G7J. She offers further resources at www.pinterest.com/pmcaloon/. Her professional site is at linkd.in/1fIRnCA.

FROM THE STREETS OF DETROIT, TO THE HILLS OF JERUSALEM, TO THE GULF OF MEXICO

By Abi Carmen

I stood there staring at the massive ship, wondering how my family had arrived at this point. There I was, 14 years old, deep in thought at Pier #39 on the West Side of New York City. My family and I were ready to board the Queen Ana Marie for a life-changing voyage to Israel. It was the beginning of a dream my mother had carried for over 30 years.

With a loving mother who cared for every one of her six children's needs and a entrepreneur father (despite that he held a Master's degree in Dream Interpretations and Analysis), we felt we were a pretty normal family, growing up in a pretty normal neighborhood on the northwest side of Detroit. Little did we know that Mom had always wanted to move to Israel. In 1969, she told Dad that he needed to sell his business within a year because she was moving there with us kids, with or without him. So there we were, at Pier #39, fulfilling my mother's dream. We were ready to embark on a voyage to a new land, a new language, and a new culture. Thus, the idea of 'following your dream' was instilled in me.

One year later in our apartment in Jerusalem, Dad was still in bed when there was a knock on the door. I answered, and a gentleman said to me in Hebrew, "I need your father to bring your mother's passport to the hospital." I relayed the message and watched as my father's face went white and he mechanically got dressed. Mother had been sick in the hospital for three weeks. I didn't know what that 5:30 a.m. visit to our apartment meant, but my father did.

A few hours later, he returned to the apartment and told us Mom had passed away. I wasn't sure what he was talking about and just looked at him. Then I walked out to our porch overlooking the hills around the Hebrew University campus and stared. I stared and stared and stared. I didn't cry. Just stared.

At 39 years old, my mom was the glue that kept our family together. Although her life was short, she had lived her dream and fulfilled it elegantly. The month before she died—although she was very sick by then—she secured us a beautiful apartment rental in Jerusalem so we could leave the cramped 250-square-foot apartment we had been cooped up in for the first year in Israel.

Life continued for me after Mom's death, through my high school years in a foreign land, foreign language, and foreign culture. This type of situation causes you to grow up pretty quickly.

A few years later I was accepted into the Pratt Institute in New York City to study architecture. I was an avid fan of Leonardo da Vinci, but I decided that five years of schooling plus five years of work in order to do what I loved was too much. I decided instead to study electronics, and I never looked back.

Then I was off to Chicago to start my first job in electronics. I spent five years at Columbia Pictures, traveling the world, running a fast-growing pinball manufacturing division. The entire time, the entrepreneurial spirit I inherited from my father was kicking into high gear. After all, my dad only lasted one year working for his older brother when he decided he needed to be his own boss.

With a leap of faith and a $10,000 bank loan, I started my first electronics service company. With a combination of my dad's entrepreneurial spirit and my mother's drive and determination for achieving a dreams, I became one of the country's largest service centers. With a customer base of individual consumers and small business owners, UAW General Motors, UAW Chrysler, the U.S. Navy, McDonald's, and many others, I thrived for the next 15 years.

I was working hard, at both my business and at home, doing home repairs and renovations on my family's farmhouse. Working hard and working hard. Wait—wasn't it supposed to be working hard and playing hard?

Meanwhile, my wife was playing hard. Our marriage fell apart, and I still can't figure out what she told my top customers to make them pull their business. But they did pull out, and I was in search of a new direction.

Go south, young man! A buddy of mine said, "We need a warmer climate, Buddy," and off we went. We drove from Chicago to Panama City Beach, Florida, for a two-week vacation, but I'm still here, 10 years later. My emotions and spirit needed the warmth, sun and new beginning just as my body needed oxygen, food, and water. Out with the windshield scrapers needed to endure Chicago winters and in with the beach sandals.

I am now at home in Destin, Florida, near some of the most beautiful, pristine, white sand beaches you'll ever see. I am far from the world of three-piece suits and matching ties.

I found a furnished condo and set up shop developing websites for local businesses. This was fun! It was more creative than electronics repair, and I met many different types of people, locals and tourists. I expanded my offerings to include e-commerce sites and began to dabble in affiliate marketing. I loved it!

My first commercial client was a cigar retailer. I probably would have built the site for free, as cigar smoking was one of my passions, but I did get paid. I knew I had found my calling, and since that first site, I have designed and developed over 160 websites in over forty-five lines of business, with each site becoming my new baby. The affiliate marketing aspect of the business fueled my understanding of the needs and desires of the different industries. Some of the fields I worked with were women's shoes, cosmetics, back pain clinics, Feng Shui, Jazz and Classical music, fitness, travel, and five different cigar companies.

I would love to discuss with every one of you how important it is to have the right mindset for what a website can accomplish; the website is the first ingredient for success. Do you want more customers? More sales? More profit? More conversions of your website traffic to actual sales? I learned that you cannot have a 'Build it and they will come' attitude. Nurturing is required in the website business, whether it's article writing, video production, search engine optimization, or social media. Every type of business needs to discover the right combination.

I am honored to help others by simplifying the process of website success. I love the opportunity to bring out Dad's entrepreneurial spirit and Mom's belief in following your dreams. It seems Dad didn't need that Master's degree in Dream Interpretation to understand what his wife wanted. He needed to just get up and do it. Show up at Pier #39 and set sail for Israel, following dreams and taking action.

ABOUT THE AUTHOR

 Abi Carmen is a business consultant specializing in Website Design & Development. With a strong background in technology, Abi uses all the tools and techniques available, including SEM (search engine marketing) and the vast array of social media offerings, to help his customers achieve their dreams, expand their online presence, and increase their profits in the ever-changing world of the Internet. With over 30 years of business experience and a passion for helping others succeed, he assist others in expanding their customer base and growing their business. To learn more about how Abi can help you and your business, please visit RedVanMedia.com and his personal website AbiCarmen.com

www.facebook.com/abicarmen

twitter.com/AbiCarmen

www.linkedin.com/in/abicarmen/

TITILLATING TITLES

By Adrienne Hew

E very online marketing course tells you to begin with keyword research.

1. Choose a niche
2. Go to Google's Keyword Planner
3. Enter a keyword to see if the niche had at least 10,000 people searching for it monthly
4. Write a report or website about any related terms that are widely searched

This is the basic formula for becoming successful online. If you did your research right, you were promised untold riches from the flood of sales as your website or blog rapidly climbed up the search engines. The process worked, but it never seemed to work quite as rapidly as we were led to believe. In fact, I often found that whatever I was working on—even if I had a passion for that niche going into it—quickly became a source of boredom and frustration.

I was trying to promote my nutrition consultancy. Unlike my competitors, my entire view of good food and nutrition doesn't boil down to fat and calories. Going after weight-loss keywords like the competition didn't feel genuine or ethical. What I know about health, weight loss, and food is so much more powerful.

I wanted to be part of the solution, not part of the problem. I wanted to set my business up to cut through all the hype and scare tactics used by my competitors. I wanted to empower my clients to understand the unchanging facts about human nutrition to find their own answers to the question, "What should I eat to be healthy?"

I had a compelling life story about my journey from debilitating illness to vibrant health. We all know that every good marketer should have one. But I was starting out with two major strikes against me: My message was extremely non-conformist, and I had no viable keywords in the eyes of Google.

Over the years, I tried different methods of monetization to reach audiences. From e-Books to full-blown courses, I explored many different ways to build revenue online, but my first successes came with Kindle publishing through Amazon.com.

In the early days, making money with this platform was easy, as new Kindle owners were frantically downloading anything they could get their hands on. I dutifully did my keyword research as the gurus taught, and plugging them into my book titles got me sales—and a few refunds, but sales nonetheless.

For a while, this got even easier when Amazon introduced their KDP Select program that would allow publishers to give away books for free for up to five days within a 90-day period. These free days would get authors many book downloads while associating them with already well-ranked books in the "Customers Who Bought This Item Also Bought" section of the Amazon page. As a result of this program, a few hundred dollars per week skyrocketed to several thousands of dollars per week.

Things were going well. My books were selling nicely, and I was making decent money online. In fact, I got so good at it that even created and sold a course in Kindle publishing, which was very well received.

Then, just like we saw with Google's Panda and Penguin algorithm updates, which knocked low-value websites out of the searches, Amazon drastically changed their algorithm to weed out the low-quality books that many of my competitors were publishing. Unfortunately, it also took down books like mine, which were previously ranking solely based on keyword research instead of links back to the page and popularity across the Internet.

I was back at square one.

At this point, I said, "F@#* it!" and decided I was just going to write what I wanted, how I wanted to. In other words, I wasn't going to write mainly based upon keyword research—popular topics, yes, just not such serious titles that only reflect keywords that people are typing into the search bar. Instead, I decided to use an angle that no one else in my marketing or nutrition circles was using: humor.

I was itching to write a book about an experience I'd had a few years prior. I was invited by a good friend to slaughter some roosters at her farm. After some stalling and insecurity about whether or not the general public would find it interesting enough to buy, I finally decided I had nothing to lose and wrote my first book in a series of funny health and nutrition titles: *50 Ways to Eat Cock: Healthy Chicken Recipes with Balls!* was born!

At first, I only showed it to a few people I knew would enjoy the tongue-in-cheek humor. Then, at the prodding of my mentor, Brad Gosse, I distributed some free copies at a marketing conference. It was an instant hit. Suddenly, I found myself signing autographs, being approached by peers who had previously shunned me, and being interviewed as an expert in creating viral titles.

Most surprising to me is how much goodwill has come my way since taking the risk of publishing this title. Now some top-level marketers are posting my title across the Internet, urging their followers to pick it up, and even coming to me for advice on naming their products and services. Others are calling me with new title ideas that I can run with for future books. And complete strangers on forums are posting positive reviews, calling it a title that "gets it right." This title has opened many doors for me, including authoring another book as a joint venture that will get the book distributed through a very lucrative catalog deal.

One of the best things with the title is that it encapsulates what I have come to understand about food and nutrition: Food is an inclusive experience around which humans have traditionally created community and fun. *50 Ways to Eat Cock* and its companion book, *50 Ways to Eat Your Honey: Recipes for Mastering the Art of Honeylingus*, make good nutrition accessible again by focusing on the fun factor. It fits in perfectly with my moniker "The Nutrition Heretic."

Let's face it. The search engines are really recommendation engines. The Internet is a big popularity contest and whoever is most popular wins. While most online marketers acknowledge that people on social media share items that make them laugh, few use humor as a means of getting more viral likes, shares, pins and re-tweets to their products and services. And great titles go viral!

Do I have detractors? Sure, I do! But you know what? I did while I was playing it safe, too. In fact, I would hazard a guess that I had more of them than I do now. The nutritional approaches I talk about are heresy to most people who have been indoctrinated in the food pyramid and low-fat mindset, but these titles give me the opportunity to open the conversation with people who have already decided they like my style.

Going back to the first Kindle course I wrote, I found that new and even established product creators and authors struggle with crafting great titles that grab their prospects' attention while branding their businesses and making more sales. Some completely fail to make a promise of what the reader will learn. Others give away too much information so that the buyers feel they already know the outcome. And still others create such bland titles that, even if the content is great, no one even notices them.

Having a strong title can make or break a sale and even reduce refund rates. I have had a total of two refunds in over eighteen months of having my bestselling titillating titles for sale. Even though my titles were always better than just plain old keyword research-driven ones, steady success didn't occur until I began writing books with titles that capture my readers' attention and imagination. In fact, the success of these titles has allowed me live out my dream of moving to Hawaii this year.

That's why today, in addition to helping people fine-tune their diets, I also show marketers and authors how to create titillating titles and marketing strategies for their products and services. Whether or not we like it, everybody judges a book by its cover and an exceptional title will make you and your book (or product or service) memorable, too.

ABOUT THE AUTHOR

Adrienne Hew, a.k.a. the Nutrition Heretic, has been called the Pope of Health and a Miracle Worker for her ability to heal disease by recommending a diet that contradicts the health gurus. Her fluency in three languages has enabled her to uncover many long forgotten food traditions throughout the world. Receiving a certificate in Chinese dietetics in 2002 and her degree as a Certified Nutritionist in 2004, she has helped many clients and workshop attendees to decode their own health dilemmas by understanding the inconsistencies in conventional nutritional dogma. As a marketer, Ms. Hew has been hailed as a thought leader in the area of comedic viral marketing. She now teaches other marketers how to build their brands by standing out from their competitors. You can learn more about her work at adriennehew.com

Connect with Adrienne at:
facebook.com/TheNutritionHeretic
twitter.com/NutriHeretic
www.linkedin.com/in/adriennehew/
plus.google.com/u/0/+AbiCarmen/posts/p/pub

READING FOR SUCCESS

By A. J. Westin

"The greatest gift is a passion for reading."
—Elizabeth Hardwick

W hen I close my eyes I can still remember like it was yesterday. It was late at night, and I was shaking all over. I was just a scared and lonely four-year-old boy holed up inside my bedroom closet, a blanket wrapped over my head, flashlight in hand, reading my favorite series of books, *Encyclopedia Brown*.

But this wasn't a happy time, not in the least. I had taken refuge in the closet to get away from the war going on between my parents down the hallway in the kitchen. My ears shook from the sound of clanging chairs as they were smashed against the wall. Angry fists pounded tables, and high-pitched voices filled the air with hate.

This is what I lived with through my entire childhood. Until fourth grade I moved seven times, including one disastrous move to the top of the Pocono Mountains in Pennsylvania while my father lived in New Jersey during the week and visited us on the weekends. Marshalls Creek was a quaint town where our nearest neighbor lived a mile away and my school was a forty-five minute drive through nowhere.

To escape this living nightmare, I lost myself in books. I couldn't get enough of them. I taught myself to read when I was three. From then on reading was my passion. It didn't matter if it was books, magazines, or newspapers—if it could be read, I read it.

Reading became a way to escape the horrors of my childhood. Science fiction was my favorite subject, and I used my imagination to visit all the places I read about. I wanted to escape the hell I was living in so badly that I imagined myself the hero, and my dreams were filled with these visions while I slept.

As much as I hated my life, I came to realize that I had the ability to write about what I was feeling as well as capturing my imagination and dreams on paper. Communicating my thoughts through writing became a way to cope with my situation at home. Writing was my outlet. It was a way for me to feel alive, to experience a life that I could only dream about.

But my life would soon change. I decided to visit one of the places of my dreams and traveled half way around the world to Hong Kong on my first-ever vacation. There I met my future wife, a Filipina working in Hong Kong. Nine months later we were married.

As with any married couple, life got in the way of my dreams. Wanting to be an author gave way to reality, and I wound up doing what both my father and my uncle did for a living—being a mailman. It wasn't the job I would have chosen but with three children to feed, there was no other choice. I had to put my dream of being an author on hold and be the kind of father I never had.

My wife had studied to be a teacher in the Philippines and finished her studies in the U.S. She taught preschool in our hometown of Neptune, New Jersey. I think it was fate that led me to marry a teacher because it set the stage for what would eventually be my life's work.

Learning begins with reading. There's no other way around it. The better reader a child is, the better they can communicate their thoughts and express themselves. Over the past 30 years, the reading comprehension of children in America has gotten progressively worse. I knew I had to do something about this, but what could I do? It was hard to compete with video games, Facebook, Twitter, and today's technology.

I remembered how my kids reacted to the stories I read them when they were very young. It wasn't just the act of reading but the types of stories that captured their imagination. I started off by reading the same books every other parent was reading but soon realized they enjoyed the stories I made up for them even more. These stories were interactive and fun and took them on adventures they looked forward to before they went to sleep.

I knew I had hit upon a formula that would help kids enjoy reading and at the same time, retain what they had read. It would be the new 3 R's Of Learning: Reading, Writing, and Retention.

Writing these stories became an obsession for me. I began talking to kids, asking them what type of stories they liked to read, what type of characters inspired them, and what they wanted in a story. The idea of influencing children in a positive way with my writing was exciting!

The first children's book I wrote was called *My Best Friend Is A Human, Really.* The story was intended to show the fun and adventure in making friends with the most unlikely people.

Friendship is an important theme and is prevalent throughout my work because it was hard for me to make friends as a child. My only friends were the characters in the books I read or made up. I wanted to show children that there were others who faced the same problems they did but overcame them in the process. From that first book, I added zombies, monsters, space aliens, superheroes, pirates, cavemen, robots, and a whole host of other weird characters to the *My Best Friend Is* series of books.

Kids have such vivid imaginations and are so inventive. Have you ever watched children act out their own stories? You can see the innocence and the joy in how they play. I wanted to capture this innocence in a way that would inspire children.

This gave me another idea which helped me take reading to the next level. Since children love to make up their own stories, I decided to put together a class to teach kids how to take those great story ideas and put them into a concise structure so they could author their own books. I named the class, "How To Write Children's Adventure Stories...So Easy a 10-Year-Old Kid Can Do It!"

As an author, my motto is, "I write books kids really want to read!" Children have been forced for so long to read just because they have to, not because they want to. You have to find a way to encourage and ignite that passion. I believe we need to give children books that inspire them.

Children are our future. They deserve our love and attention. In Luke 11:11-12, Jesus speaks about how we should treat one another. He says, "What father among you, if his son asks for a fish, will instead of a fish give him a serpent; or if he asks for an egg, will give him a scorpion? Are we giving the best for our children?

I am dedicated to helping children become better readers. The Merriam-Webster definition of literacy is the ability to read and write. That's not good enough for me. I want to take it even further. Literacy should be defined as the ability to read, write, and understand as well as to communicate the written and spoken word.

The better a child is able to read, the better the odds for a successful and productive life. These are words I live by, and after having gone through a lifetime of pain and neglect, the Lord has prepared me for this calling. In John 13:34, Jesus says, "Love one another as I have loved you." I love children so much and the lasting legacy I want to give them is my gift of the written word.

ABOUT THE AUTHOR

A. J. Westin is a best-selling children's book author who has written over two-dozen books. He's known as "The Adventure Book Guy" and has inspired countless children throughout the world with his tales of fun and adventure and is a leading advocate for literacy in America. His vision is to see children not only become great readers but great writers and this can be found in his newest project, "How To Write Children's Adventure Stories... So Easy a 10 Year Old Kid Can Do It!" You can find this and all his children's books on his website at: www.ajwestin.com.

Connect with A.J. at:

facebook.com/ajwestinauthor

twitter.com/ajwestin33

plus.google.com/111918714410215208965

DON'T LIMIT YOUR CHALLENGES, CHALLENGE YOUR LIMITS

By Dr. Gala Gorman, CPA

My partner and I sat at our favorite restaurant for about the hundredth time. Every Thursday for many years, we took the afternoon to mastermind…and just enjoy each other's company. We knew we needed to work on our business with the same enthusiasm that we worked in our business. That time we set aside every week ensured our success, and by most standards we were successful.

A problem had been brewing for several years, though. The solutions I was designing, for us and for our clients, failed to inspire me. Even though every situation was a bit different, life had become monotonous. It was a personal crisis that felt liberating in an odd way.

Let me digress. At the time, I felt that I didn't really know who I was. If my name had not been on my platinum American Express card and I didn't have a sense that the bill would be paid (thanks to my reliable and healthy salary), I would really have felt like no one, or anyone.

It wasn't that I was really lonely; I had companionship. I wasn't isolated; I was around people. It was a lack of passion and purpose in my work that was stoking this fire. As a student of metaphysics for many years, I was quite used to deep contemplation. Still, being stuck in the same rut for over a decade had taken its toll. I knew I needed a change, so I began taking extended vacations during our slow season.

The previous year, I had traveled with a friend through Europe. After processing the amazing experiences from that trip and working my way through another tax season, I realized it was time for me to consider the next adventure in my journey.

I asked my friend, the same friend who had accompanied me to Europe the year before, if she was game for another adventure. Her interest was piqued when I told her she could pick the place since I had chosen Europe. She had been thinking about a trip to Brazil. To her surprise, I said, "Great. Where do we sign up?" A few months later, we were on our way to Rio de Janeiro.

We were to stay in a community in the hills outside Rio. I had no idea what to expect, since I didn't know much about the country, its people, or the spiritual practices that the community was organized around.

We took a bus from the Rio airport, riding in the front seats to take in the lovely view. It felt like a perfect start to the next phase of the journey. I thought, Maybe that's what this experience is supposed to feel like—having front row seats!

We arrived at our destination and were greeted warmly. We were part of a group of 20 or so people from North America who had come to join the community's annual festivities and experience a spiritual journey. It was a vision quest of sorts.

We were shown to our room in one of the nicer buildings on the property. I would sleep on a futon on a platform several inches off the ground. My friend had a mattress on the floor. With no linens, we used our sleeping bags. The window was always open. We shared our room with lizards and an enormous spider. Rio was experiencing a severe drought. Water was trucked in for necessities only.

Others from our group were assigned to homes all over the community. Several people I became close with were staying at the top of a hill. Because of their location, they were first to accumulate rainwater. Hence, they actually had a shower. I would pack a small bag and hike up 63 steep steps carved into the jungle to use their shower. It wasn't hot, but as an alternative to no shower at all, it was bliss.

Not long into this experience, I told my friend that I would not stay until we were supposed to depart in three weeks. How long could I live in these conditions? And I needed to stay until I discovered what I came to experience, but I couldn't imagine that taking so long.

But then we spent the next two weeks living and loving life more fully than I had ever known possible. We came to love our meager surroundings and didn't miss the comforts of home. Those comforts came in a distant second to the feeling of home that I was experiencing.

By the time our journey came to an end, I was the one who wasn't ready to leave. Still, I understood that I needed to take what I had learned home with me and apply it to my life. I had changed in profound ways. The only way to fully understand those changes was to go back to the life I had left behind several weeks before.

Shortly after my return from Brazil, I told my partner I was ready for a new experience. After 20 years working in financial services, I was ready to walk away from the accounting firm. It didn't seem fair to him to linger in my comfortably uncomfortable position, knowing I wasn't fully committed to what we were working to build. In what seemed like an almost effortless negotiation, I sold my half of the company to my partner, and the deal was closed within a few months.

Of course, that ending was just the beginning! I had the time to pursue my interests and passion for practical spirituality. I have authored several books in the *Spiritual Approach* series^{TM}. I also earned a Doctoral Ministerial Degree with an emphasis on Life Coaching.

As you work to sharpen your skills in any endeavor, it is likely you will be given more challenging material to work with. The adversity you experience tests your character. You get to see what you're made of. As a result, you challenge yourself to be a little better next time.

The road I've traveled since selling my company has had its fair share of challenges. I experience the turbulence of life much differently now. After a momentary relapse—also known as wallowing—I started looking for the perfection in the experience.

You wouldn't want to take a roller coaster ride that didn't get your heart racing. Well, life is that ride. It's up to us to find the joy in every twist and turn of the roller coaster and to know when it's time to float on the lazy river. If you would like to tag along as I seek to squeeze the zest from life, you can find me at www.DrGala.com.

ABOUT THE AUTHOR

Dr. Gala Gorman, CPA, is an entrepreneur—a holistic life coach, publisher, business consultant, real estate broker, metaphysical minister, and formerly an accounting firm partner. She draws from all of her endeavors in her authored works.

The lines blur when moving from business management to life management; they are two sides of the same coin. In her words, "It's the business of your life and you're the CEO."

As a student of Eastern and Western philosophy, she works to infuse a blend of the best of both worlds—what she refers to as practical spirituality—into business and life.

Dr. Gala has authored articles and books on holistic methods for solving both personal and business difficulties. She gained popularity as a teacher, speaker, and coach by sharing the methods that have served her well over the years.

Would you like to know what Dr. Gala considers essential tools for the journey of life? Visit www.DrGala.com/SWDYD for immediate access to her free report Building Your Spiritual Tool Chest™.

You can learn more about Dr. Gala at:

www.Amazon.com/Gala-Gorman/e/B00EG8Y2EW
www.Facebook.com/DrGalaAuthor
www.Goodreads.com/DrGalaAuthor
www.Linkedin.com/in/GalaGorman/
Twitter.com/DrGalaAuthor

SOMETIMES LIFE THROWS YOU A CURVE BALL

By Candy L. Hill

I t was the summer of 1979, and I was home on a two-week break before starting my second year of graduate school. I had not been home since Christmas, so I spent a lot of time with my family. One night I had dinner out with my maternal grandmother, who turned 79 that July. She asked about school and my plans for the future.

My mother and I also visited her at home that week. She had bought a cute three-room house in town after my grandfather died. They had lived about thirty-five minutes away, and she wanted to be closer to everything. She looked so rested and healthy that night. I figured she would live at least another decade. I was wrong.

Later that night we got a call from the local police department. We had to go to Yale-New Haven Hospital right away. Something was wrong with my grandmother.

We flew down the turnpike—I don't remember ever going so fast—and got to the hospital in record time. A policeman, doctor, nurse, and priest met us, so we knew it was not good. My mother asked for my grandmother, but they said they wanted to talk to us first.

They told us there had been a break-in at my grandmother's house and that she had been badly beaten. The police thought she might have woken up, and the burglars were afraid she recognized one of them. He probably got scared and strangled her. She was pronounced dead at the scene.

I don't remember much after that except that I wanted to see her. They said it wasn't a good idea, as she had been so badly beaten. My mother wondered if they were sure it was my grandmother. The nurse, who was a neighbor to my grandmother, identified her. I still regret not seeing her one last time.

The next few days were a blur. My sister and her husband came home from Delaware. One of my aunts said that we were going to have to live with this for the rest of our lives. She was right, of course. Thirty-five years later it still affects me. It changed all our lives.

Police caught the two perpetrators. They were prosecuted and convicted. They are out now; I heard one is married and has a family.

I returned to grad school a couple of weeks later and basically slept for the next six months. I would get up, go to class, teach, and go home and back to bed. It was how I coped with the stress.

I completed my Master's degree in December 1981 and honored my teaching contract through June of the following year. My plan had been to complete my doctorate and teach at the college level, but after my grandmother's death, I did not feel I could handle the stress of qualifying exams and prelims. I went home and sold shoes for year or so while looking for a "real" job.

One evening in the fall of 1983, my stepfather had a tire blowout on I-95. As he waited for the tow truck, a family friend drove by and pulled up behind my stepfather's truck. They talked while waiting for the tow truck, and he told my stepfather that his sister had a job opening. She was looking for someone who could read and write. He thought I should call her, so I did.

It was a Research Assistant position in the Department of Psychiatry at Yale University. We met and talked for an hour. She kept saying I was over-qualified, and my response was, "I'm selling shoes, making $9,000 a year, please give me a chance." She agreed and scheduled me to meet with the director and associate director of the unit. They offered me the job, and I started on October 10, 1983.

I was there for 10 years, and over the years I worked my way up to research administrator. I learned many things and held an array of responsibilities. I worked closely with one doctor for many years. Together we led a number of anxiety groups, which was a lot like teaching. I also saw a few individual patients and managed the clinical trials. After five years, my boss said that my talents were in administration, and it was time for me to give up the patient contact. My last five years were spent administering all of the grants and clinical trials.

In 1993, I moved to Gainesville, Florida, with a psychiatrist and a nurse I worked with at Yale. The three of us started a psychiatric specialty clinic in the Department of Psychiatry at the University of Florida. A few years later we moved to the chairman's office. In 2004, I was promoted to Assistant Director of Research for the Department of Psychiatry and currently occupy that position in two departments in the College of Medicine.

Throughout my tenure at UF, I often felt that this was not really what I wanted to do with my life. I was bored and unhappy. But I stayed, mainly out of fear.

Then my boss was asked to teach a grant-writing course to grad students, scheduled to start January 2009. He asked if I wanted to teach it with him. Of course I said yes! The class was quite successful and we were asked to teach it again in January 2011. The class has been so popular that we have been teaching it annually ever since. This year's class, our fifth, was the largest yet—twenty-one students. Recently my boss told me that he would not teach this class without me—a high compliment indeed. Teaching this class is often the highlight of my week!

Fortunately I have interests outside of my job. I started my first business in the late 1990s, making and selling handmade bead jewelry locally under the name Sweet Creations - Jewelry by Candy. Photography has been a part of my life for as long as I can remember as well. In 2009, I helped found a photography club. I started an online gallery in 2010 and a photoblog, clhPhotography, in 2012.

Two years ago I decreased my work hours so I could start developing a consulting business. I started researching my next move. I discovered NAMS in late 2012, and it was the impetus I needed. I have learned so much and I think I am ready to move on in my life. I even began a blog on starting a small business called On The Right Path because it aptly describes how I feel.

Throughout my career I have served as an editor and copywriter. All grants in our department must go through me for review and revision. My friend tells me I can spot a typo at 20 paces. I have found typos or errors on some of the most professional websites. I plan to offer proofreading and copyediting help to online businesses and online marketing, as well as teaching copyediting basics.

ABOUT THE AUTHOR

 Candy L. Hill was born and raised in the New Haven, Connecticut area. She attended Eastern Connecticut State College, where she received a Bachelor of Arts degree in Sociology and Applied Social Relations. After graduation she attended Iowa State University and earned her Master of Science degree in Sociology. Candy currently lives and works in Gainesville, Florida, where she has been for over 20 years.

Photography has been a part of Candy's life for as long as she can remember. You can find her photos at clh-photography.com as well as on Flickr, ViewBug, and 500x. Prior to attending Iowa State, Candy had never been west of New Jersey. Since moving to Florida, however, she has traveled a lot, including a Mediterranean cruise in 2009 that was the trip of her lifetime. She took over 1,500 photos during the 10-day cruise. Candy's copyediting business can be found at clhConsulting.com. She is also working on showcasing her jewelry online.

Connect with Candy at:

www.facebook.com/clhConsulting

twitter.com/CandyLHill

www.linkedin.com/in/candylhill/

plus.google.com/u/0/+CandyLHill/

LITTLE THINGS MATTER

By Rachel Martin

suppose I could just tell you that I'm a blogger, website owner, speaker, podcaster, and start-up owner. You might smile and nod and think I'm a little crazy for doing so much. But that's what I do, not why I do what I do. To know me, you need to understand the why behind me and get a glimpse into my heart.

I've made my share of mistakes, I've fallen down, and I've spent time wondering "now what?" as tears filled my eyes. I'm a mother to seven amazing kids. My kids have taught me more about joy, patience, perseverance, and maintaining a sense of wonder than I could have learned from all the books in any bookstore. I love speaking and sharing my heart with others. I'm an artist in crazy ways—with piano keys under my fingers, in my garden beds, and through my computer keys, as my thoughts spill out into sentences, paragraphs, and articles.

I am also a partner in an amazing company called Blogging Concentrated, for which I travel the country teaching bloggers to be their best, make money, determine goals and dreams for their businesses, and implement them. I write a website called Finding Joy, and my words reach millions.

You also need to know I was a slave to fear for many years, but in the last years of my life, I've decided that fear has no place in determining joy, happiness, and success. Now, instead of asking "Why?" I choose to ask "Why not?"

You're probably thinking that I must not sleep much. Or you're wondering how I do it all. I always respond to that with the truth: coffee. In reality, though, beyond my love of lattes, I am simply blessed to do work that I love.

You see, for much of my adult life, I lived with the philosophy that "if this happens/gets fixed/etc., then I will be happy." I was living life on hold, letting fear hold me back, waiting for life to give me ideal circumstances. As we all know, time doesn't slow down, even for my if/then philosophy. Time moves—exponentially.

One January day in 2011, I found myself choosing to really live and embrace life despite not having the if part figured out. That was the winter my youngest son, Samuel, was diagnosed with Celiac Disease. Celiac Disease destroys the small intestine of an individual who eats gluten, which is found in wheat, barley, rye, and sometimes oats. Since the intestines are destroyed, no nutrients are able to pass, and the person suffering from Celiac Disease essentially starves.

Samuel had been fading away for months, and at fifteen-months old, he was in the hospital, very weak, and finally diagnosed with Celiac Disease. As relieved as I was for a diagnosis, my momma's heart was filled with fear of the unknown, fear of more issues, and an ache for my baby sleeping in the hospital bed next to me. I tell you humbly, on that night tears streamed down my face.

They were tired tears, tears of a momma fighting. Tears of a momma watching her vibrant boy fade away in front of her. They were tears of fear. Then, as the snow fell outside the window of Children's Hospital in Minneapolis, I heard the sound that changed my life.

Beep. Beep. Beep. It was Samuel's heart monitor. His heart was beating with a beautiful, steady rhythm. I knew in that moment to be profoundly grateful, as there were moms and dads in that same hospital who would have done anything for the steady sound of a normal heartbeat. I started to list everything I was grateful for: the IV in his hand, nurses who laughed with me and hugged me and listened, a cot for me to sleep in, a bag of gluten-free snacks. I was no longer waiting for an if/then reason to be grateful. Instead, on that snowy evening, I threw out the qualifiers and simply found a bit of joy in the difficult.

That gratitude became my voice in everything I do. It became the backbone behind my website and it determines how I parent. It's also reflected in my company, Blogging Concentrated. It's not always as simple as listing everything for which I am joyful, but rather it's about being very aware of the gift of today, while also planning for tomorrow and being grateful for the past.

As time went on, my site grew exponentially. I began writing Dear Mom letters—simple letters about the trials and emotions of motherhood—and as I wrote more, the demand grew. After all, with seven children of my own, I had plenty of firsthand experience in mothering. I had a very specific goal to acknowledge the challenges of motherhood but to ultimately inspire, motivate, and challenge mothers to carry on.

I began writing about the wonder in normal, everyday life, about the crazy gift of mothering, and about moments and time. I truly challenged other mothers not to dismiss their worth but to see the amazing in what often feels mundane. You see, no matter our profession, our story, or our life dreams, we all live a journey filled with ordinary, normal moments. Sprinkled among the normal moments are bits of beauty and joy that we'll celebrate as the years of our lives tick away.

Letting go of my fear allowed me to see those joyful moments. It meant I would stand in front of hundreds, tell them my story, and encourage them to not allow fear, expectations, or the imperfect life keep them from living fully today. Letting go of fear meant making hard choices. It meant saying, "I am enough," and then writing those words for moms all over the world to read.

As my blog grew, so did the opportunities. I began writing for The Huffington Post, published nationally-syndicated articles, and secured a book deal for my own book, *Dear Mom Letters*. I became a partner in Blogging Concentrated, which I love and believe in. My business partner, Dan R. Morris (who is published in the first edition of *So What Do You Do?*), and I are passionate about equipping, inspiring, and teaching bloggers to look at their websites as a business and to use them as a stepping stone to greater financial freedom. We present our workshops all over the country, manage a monthly membership site, create curriculum, speak at blogging/social media events, and are very busy doing what we love. I get to stand in front of a room of blogging professionals and remind them that every post, every word, every podcast, and every video is a ripple in this journey of life. Those ripples change lives.

It's hard for me to end a presentation without tears in my eyes because I know we all have an innate capability to change lives through our words, actions, and choices. I look at my own life and am simply humbled. I'm grateful for the courage to sit in front of the computer and type the reflections of my heart onto a screen and then to hit 'publish.' I'm grateful for opportunities and great friends.

Sometimes, in the business sphere, we can forget to be grateful for the mundane little things, even though those little things are truly some of life's greatest gifts. So embrace today. Love the little things. Tell those you love that you love them. Don't let life pass by. It's not really about me; it's about a world of possibility and finding joy.

ABOUT THE AUTHOR

Rachel Martin, is the writer behind the site FindingJoy.net, is a partner of BloggingConcentrated.com, is cofounder of the Amplify Podcast, and is a featured writer for The Huffington Post. Rachel has built a site with millions of visitors, and has created a successful ebook campaign resulting in her first book the "Dear Mom Letters". Her articles have been featured on Huffington

Post, PopSugar, iVillage, SheKnows, Parents.com, WhattoExpect, Dr. Greene, Blogher, National Foundation for Celiac Disease, and more. In it all Rachel believes in living each day intentionally and loves working with others to help cultivate vision and potential.

Connect with Rachel at:

facebook.com/findingjoyblog

twitter.com/finding_joy

www.linkedin.com/pub/rachel-martin/59/6a1/a90/

plus.google.com/u/1/+RachelMartin/posts

AN INCH WIDE
AND A MILE DEEP

By Jeff Herring

H ave you ever been told you couldn't do something? If you're anything like me, being told that makes me want to do it more, to prove that I can.

Travel with me to 1986. I'm trying to finish my Ph.D. in Family Therapy at Florida State. It's not going well. Everything I write is rejected. They hand something back to me to correct, and I correct it. Then they return that, asking me to correct it to its original form. A couple professors began to suggest that perhaps I just couldn't write.

Then, while waiting in the secretary' office, I took the opportunity to sneak a look at my file. My favorite professor in the Counseling Psychology Master's program wrote the following in her letter of recommendation to the doctoral program in Family Therapy: "Jeff is a great student, works well with clients, and is very personable. While I am happy to recommend him for the doctoral program, my concern is in his ability to express himself with the written word. This may become a challenge at the dissertation level."

Well, that was all I needed to learn—I can't write!—and I never did finish my Ph.D. Instead, I built a thriving private practice, my way of saying, "So there!"

Fast forward to fall 1994. The local newspaper had been asking local therapists to contribute to a mental health column. Each therapist got to submit a weekly column for six months to a year.

They wrote about incredibly interesting (catch the sarcasm) topics such as, "What is Depression?" and "What is Bi-Polar Disorder?" I decided I could do better than that. I applied the next time around. I didn't get it, furthering my belief that I could not write.

Being a persistent fellow, however, I tried again the next time the opening came around. That time I got it! My first thought was, how am I going to come up with a new topic every week? Oh well, it's only for six months or a year. I'll figure something out.

I simply wrote in conversational language about the problems I saw in my office and how we made things better. That gig lasted for twenty years. I discovered there is something magical about helping people understand how to approach and solve their problems.

The column filled my practice with clients. When the newspaper went online, I began to get clients from all over the country. Every other therapist in town was being asked, "How much do you charge and will my insurance cover it?" I was being asked, "How soon can we get in to see you, Jeff?"

It would nice to tell you that everyone lived happily ever after and life was all great from then on, but it wouldn't be true. For eleven years, I used this newfound ability to build a thriving private practice, all the while staring another great therapy niche in the face without really seeing it.

People said to me, "Jeff, you're a really good therapist, but you're an even a better writer. You need to teach this online!" Folks kept telling me that I should teach this "column-writing stuff" to people online. I kept thinking it sounded good, but there is only so much newspaper space. Why train my competition?

Finally, in October 2005, I launched my first web site and online courses teaching content creation. It went very well, but I was also distracted by my divorce during the same time. The divorce was expected, but I didn't expect that my boys' mother would move them from Tallahassee to Atlanta.

Deciding not to put our boys in the middle of a big fight, I choose to move to Atlanta as well. I spent that year cramming a week's worth of clients into three days in Tallahassee, then driving to Atlanta for the rest of the week to see my boys and get my business started there. I repeated that hectic schedule each week for all of 2006.

Christmas Eve found me sleeping in a hotel lobby in Atlanta. I stayed in the lobby because I could not afford to get a room, after a year's worth of back-and-forth, living in two cities and paying for two households. Something important happened in the wee hours of that night. I decided I would get so good at something that everyone online needed—that is, content creation—so that I would never be in that financial situation again.

I went online full-time in February 2007, and things really began to take off. In just over a year, I went from making about $200 a month online to making more than $20,000 a month. I discovered something critically important along the way: when you go an inch wide and a mile deep into your niche, two very cool things happen:

1. You discover things that no one else has discovered before, and
2. You create things that no one else has created before.

One of the most powerful things I discovered was that content marketing allows you to master the five factors for online success in any niche:

1. Content Creation: unleashing your content and making a difference in the world

2. Online Visibility: getting found online and being seen as the go-to expert in your niche, without having to be online all the time

3. Traffic Generation: creating waves of high-quality traffic from your ideal clients

4. List Building: growing a highly responsive list of gold, eager to invest in your products and services

5. Product Creation: cashing in on your content by creating resources and services that your prospects will invest in and love.

By going an inch wide and a mile deep, I created a powerful process called "Five Simple Steps to Six-Figure Success" in any niche. The nice thing about having a proven and time-tested system like this is that it insulates you from "shiny object syndrome." If it doesn't fit into one of the five simple steps and it's not going to help you build your business right away, you don't need it.

It's a joy to get up every morning knowing I get to spend my day helping great people get their life-changing message out to the world. And remember this: There are more people out there waiting to hear your unique message, who can hear it from only you, than you can ever get to in your lifetime. Go use this stuff!

ABOUT THE AUTHOR

Jeff Herring has been building his own businesses with Content Marketing since 1994. With his exclusive Content Marketing strategies, Jeff has fast become a Living Legend of Quality Traffic Generation. Crowned "The King of Content Marketing by Entrepreneur Magazine, Jeff has long been the "behind the scenes" guy creating Direct Response Content for many top internet marketers and business leaders, with clients such as Dan Kennedy, Alex Mandossian and others.

Jeff is going to show you a simple yet powerful system for creating prospect & profit pulling content in 20 minutes or less…

Visit JeffHerring.com to learn how.

Connect with Jeff at:

facebook.com/jeffherringmarketing

twitter.com/jeffherring

www.linkedin.com/in/articlemarketing

A SEMINAL UPBRINGING

by Charlsa Perdew

grew up in a small Alabama town in the 1960s. This was a town where, in the sogginess of a July morning, a neighbor might holler to my mama through the wooden screen door, "Martha, you busy?" And in the door she'd come to sit and have a cup of coffee, just to visit. Nothing more, no agenda other than "visiting." There was talk of the garden and vacation Bible school plans, babies, Brownie Girl Scout Day Camp, nicked knees, and grocery store sales.

My summers were filled with grass-stained knees and elbows, baseball cards in bicycle spokes, special days at the city pool where big kids jumped off the high dive, and where a quarter would buy a PayDay bar. Nights were cricket-crested playgrounds with the kids on the street, playing "kick the can" and catching lightning bugs in mayonnaise jars with ice-pick holes poked in the lids. Little cotton window curtains fluttered slightly on the nights when the heat was tolerable. The train whistle broke the heavy stillness at predictable intervals. It was a good town.

But when August was just about over and school started again after Labor Day, the talk changed, and the sounds of the night became more

63

magical than even the most stellar summer evening could offer. The open windows carried the beat of drums—big, loud, deep poundings accompanying the strains of marching band practice—faint but discernible nonetheless. Football season was upon us.

Alabama never had much to brag about. The state as a whole carried a great burden of embarrassing, pock-marked events during that time period. Still today, I shudder at the memory of hatred and fear that marks the history of the Deep South and, of course, other states as well. We didn't really know we were backward; we just knew what we knew. Our little town integrated without incident, and I was too young to notice anything abnormal about it at all. I didn't know how high the cost had been. I didn't know.

It's this kind of history, I believe, that brought us to such a reverence for football. We seemed to crave something positive on which to hang our hats, something at which we could excel, something at which we were the gold standard, rather than the brunt of the latest jokes.

In our state, you have to choose. It is a given. Everyone makes his or her choice. When I was a kid, families were for one team or the other. When mentioning a family in passing, you might hear, "Oh, sure, they're Auburn," or "Oh yeah, they're Alabama. Always have been." Our high school was diplomatic in choosing team colors and a name. The colors were red and white (for Alabama) and the mascot was a Tiger (for Auburn)—a brilliant compromise!

On Friday nights, we sat under Army blankets on cold, concrete bleacher seats, sipping hot chocolate from glass Thermos bottles and cheering for the Tigers. We knew the names of all the players, where they went to church and who their folks were. I thought their girlfriends were the luckiest gals in the world. They were heroes to us, win or lose. We loved them.

I was a tomboy. I liked to play with the boys on our street, to throw the football and pretend that the game was accessible to the likes of me, a girl. My daddy loved football, and I loved my daddy. My mama grew up an Alabama fan, so we were Alabama fans as a family as well.

I was about six years old when Daddy got sick. He died when I was 10. Mama moved my sister and me to a new house with a yard full of pine trees that always needed raking in the fall. We'd set up the transistor radio, leaning against a tree on those autumn Saturday afternoons and listen to Alabama football games while we piled up and burned that pine straw. I can still hear the sounds, even now—the crowd and the play-by-play guy that brought the game to life and out of that little radio box.

Sunday mornings at church were glorified or tainted by the win or loss of the day before. And if the ultimate game of the year—Alabama vs. Auburn—had been played the day before, children either happily anticipated or dreaded those few moments before Sunday school when they could gloat or eat crow over the game's outcome.

This was the pond in which I swam. It will forever impact me, no matter where I live, work, or vacation. I will always be an Alabama fan.

As a young adult, I moved away to the big city—Atlanta, Georgia. My team did not do well during those years. I discovered that any outward response to the jabs of colleagues was incentive for them to continue the taunts. So in the heart of Bulldog and Yellow Jacket country, I became a closeted 'Bama fan. I rooted for the Braves and the Hawks and went to their games, but for twenty-three years I held back my enthusiasm for football.

And then…I moved back to Alabama. I immediately headed to the DMV to purchase an Alabama vanity license plate ("PKYDRM," which stood for Big Al, Alabama's elephant mascot) and to renew season ticket applications.

It didn't take long to feel the familiar loyalty. Everywhere we looked there were Alabama hats and signs and t-shirts. It felt good. The team? Well, not so great, actually. We were under NCAA sanctions and restrictions involving scholarship reductions and probationary rules. The once-mighty program was ravaged by the folly and arrogance of a coach who embarrassed the program. An experienced coach wouldn't take the position. We waited as the time ticked by.

It turned out to be worth the wait: celebrated former national championship coach Nick Saban joined us. Wow! It felt as if the State of Alabama had been issued a doomsday reprieve! We stopped saying, "Remember when?" and looked toward the future. I wanted a part in the big picture of college football under this spell of renewed hope.

My husband and I went to see the movie *Julie and Julia*, about a young woman who began to blog about Julia Child's French recipes. That gave me an idea! Women in the south loved football, but as a whole knew very little about the game. I decided to write a blog to teach women about college football. Followers could ask questions, and I'd answer. We'd start at square one and build from there.

My husband and I brainstormed, and we began. I researched answers to questions and read articles. I asked questions of my friends who had played college ball.

Then I was asked to do a workshop, so I assembled a PowerPoint and set my fees. Local radio featured the blog on their website and sports talk personalities took my calls on air. Week by week the blog grew and information was assembled. At the end of that season, I had the core of my first e-Book, *Let's Kick it Off, Ladies!*

In truth, I am a small-town girl who returned to her roots and found a way to share something novel and fun. I know that somewhere this season, a woman's football knowledge might just make a man's head turn toward her in wonder! Sweet.

Please visit us at www.southerngirlscollegefootballguide.com.

ABOUT THE AUTHOR

Charlsa Taul Perdew served as a vocal music educator in metropolitan Atlanta for more than thirteen years and was Adjunct Professor of Music at Georgia State University. Charlsa holds Master's Degrees in Education and Vocal Performance from the Universities of Alabama and Georgia State.

Employed by the Atlanta Opera Chorus for thirteen seasons, she twice served as mezzo soprano soloist with Atlanta Opera Studio. Via

Atlanta Opera's Artist/Mentor Program she wrote curriculum guides for music camps at Atlanta's FOX THEATRE.

She directed eight State Champion vocal ensembles. Charlsa was named Teacher of the Year at the Cobb Center for the Performing Arts. Her choirs have performed at Carnegie Hall and Westminster Abby and were featured on demos by SHAWNEE PRESS.

Currently, Charlsa maintains a private vocal studio and is Conductor/Artistic Director for the choir, CANTANTI DELLA DONNA.

Her passion and love for college football led her to write *Let's Kick it Off Ladies* and to blog about Southern football.

twitter.com/charlsat

INSIDE-OUT REINVENTION

By Bryan Harnois

T he glass pendant was glowing brightly at over 3000 degrees as it flew like a meteor across the studio and shattered into large pieces against the concrete floor. Through misty eyes I watched and listened as the chunks cooled rapidly, crackling and snapping as the stresses set up within tore them apart.

My thoughts raced. Emotions washed and crashed over me in waves. What was the point? Why was I bothering to make yet another beautiful bauble?

Realization swept over me that my retirement dreams were crumbling around me just as my art lay in ruins before me.

I was born in the mid-fifties and raised in a working class family, my childhood fairly typical for many Boomers. We kids ate simple healthy food, played outdoors from sunup to sundown, studied hard and were generally well and happy.

We weren't poor but money was tightly budgeted. There was no budget for Health Care costs, no health care plan, no regular visits to the Doctor. The only house call I remember was when I had the chickenpox so badly I had itchy poxes on poxes, and my parents were in great distress over my fevered hallucinations. Our 'Health Care System' kicked in, and the extended family matriarchs collaborated on the phone party-line, but no common sense solution was forthcoming. The General Practitioner was summoned, laid on gentle hands, diagnosed pneumonia, a potion was dispensed and reassuring words were murmured. I recovered. The kind words my parents had about our experience with this now anonymous healer have remained with me.

My parents life goal was helping their kids transcend from the lives of labor that were the norm for our family tree, into educated professionals with a better future. I excelled in school, my technically oriented mind largely molded by my science teacher, an amateur photographer who saw in me an artistic side. As a teen I took to nature photography under his mentorship as a way to express myself.

Driven by my passion, I sold my parents on letting me work one summer as an arcade game caller at the local carnival, earning enough to buy a great camera. I leveraged that investment into my first business, taking photos at sports tournaments and then spending the night printing proofs to presell orders the next day. The tight production schedule demanded efficiency, and the seeds of my passion for self-management, systems and teamwork were sown.

The winter of 1973 I was fast tracking to a career as a science teacher, when I applied to Med School on a dare from a friend: he would apply if I did. I had already briefly considered a career in Medicine. I liked counseling and teaching people and the dare rekindled memories of the GP who had saved my life. It was game on.

That summer I worked in the wood yard of my hometown's paper mill as a log jockey, stacking tons of logs over the course of the three summers I was employed there to help pay for my education. I remember coming home bruised and dirty from work and my parents meeting me at the door with an envelope emblazoned with the Med school's logo. We all just stood and stared at it for the longest time, apprehension palpable, the smell of fear in the air. When I finally dared to open it, I danced for joy with Mom, then realized Dad was just standing there, tears running down his cheeks, staring at the letter. A journey was launched. My family and I were reinventing our future.

Fast-forward seven years to when I started a private practice as a young Family Doctor with Big Ideas. My Residency had trained me in a Holistic Team-based approach to providing Health and Wellness care and the vision of making a difference in peoples wellness was intoxicating.

Much to the bemusement of my more established colleagues, I promptly attempted to put that leading-edge model into play in the real world of the office, the hospital wards and the ER. Harsh reality soon reared its ugly head. It quickly became clear that the Cadillac model of the training program was not really completely implementable in the Pontiac world of a publicly funded health care system. My wife and I learned to accept the personal financial limitations imposed by the high overhead of running a Wellness focused practice. The model of care made sense to us and we were sustained by my core belief of Medicine as a Privileged Calling and a life of service.

However two decades later I was working in excess of 80 hours a week, trading my time for money. My life was unbalanced and despite my ideals something had to change, so I transitioned to full time ER work and helped co-create the best team I've ever worked with. My wellness mentoring continued in a form adapted to the ER, often achieving 'a-ha' moments for patients around wellness issues. This evolution afforded us financial stability and I had more time to reengage with the pro-bono consulting work I did with wellness workers to build their businesses.

Most significantly I had more time for my creative pursuits, including photography, woodturning and glassblowing. I now invested heavily in growing my skills in the wood and glass shops. I enjoyed everything about the shops: working with my hands, practicing eye-hand and muscle memory skills, the smell of aromatic woods and the all enveloping heat of the glass shop on frigid winter days. I was in 'the zone' when creating there.

I began to envision building an Artisan business for my eventual retirement, making my art and selling it to the tourists who come to our ocean playground on the East Coast every year. A business plan was hatched, tested, and seemed viable. Everything seemed on track to reinvention into a fulfilling working retirement that would see us reasonably secure.

The financial melt down in 2009 changed everything. Our investments were damaged and the local tourism economy was also badly diminished. I began to worry that my dream business was on the ropes before it really got started.

The full reality of the situation hit home that January day in 2010 when something in me shattered and in despair I hurled my beautiful pendant in a meteoric arc to its destruction.

At that point the evolution of my reinvention was halted. What immediately replaced it was…. nothing. For a month or so I looked within myself for answers, but none were forthcoming. I worked diligently in the ER, but didn't go near my workshops.

I finally found strength in wellness principles I had taught for years, renewing the meditative practice I had let lapse and engaging with a life coach. In the process I had my horizons expanded to more of the marvelous wellness work being down outside of medicine.

My business plan was revisited, leading me to conclude that I needed to eliminate my total dependence on seasonal tourist traffic and figure out how to take this business online. Being a techie computer geek since the 1970's how difficult could this online marketing thing really be?

I set out to reinvent myself once again, this time as an online marketer.

My search for a mentor led to Rich Schefren, a Strategic Systems-based business builder. Our early inner work focused on the importance of identifying and working in your core strengths, and clarified I had actually been doing so in my clinical, creative and entrepreneurial work for decades, I just hadn't thought of it that way: I was a strategic system and team builder, a collator of information into easily teachable formats and a lifelong teacher, my style that of a somewhat quirky no-BS mentor.

As I moved forward along my internet marketing path, I also came to clarity on how vital such a deep inner exploration is to setting oneself up to grow a business. A light bulb went on. I realized that my envisioned reinvention goal was skewed and that my why was not all about transitioning to making and marketing my art in a self-serving model, but was still rooted in service and centered on helping people optimize their wellness, just on a bigger scale.

While my vision of a business based totally in my artistic passion proved less than viable, and shattered that January day, through the resulting inner exploration I discovered not only the core strengths and the stories within me required to expand the reach of my consulting and coaching with wellness promoters, but also the fundamental importance of this deep inner exploration to anyone wishing to build an expertise based business.

While this inner exploration can be difficult, and goes beyond just mindset, doing the work upfront under the guidance of someone experienced in the process can make everything else in growing your business easier and more rewarding in the long term.

Today, I mentor Wellnesspreneurs and other creatives in deeply exploring and reinventing their inner expertise, transforming their creative solutions to their ideal client's problems into the business they envision and the lifestyle they desire, leading to security, self fulfillment and contribution to the greater good.

ABOUT THE AUTHOR

Bryan Harnois M.D. is an entrepreneur, ER clinician and creative who still blows glass recreationally.

His unconventional thinking on business building and wellness delivery produces resources and automation leveraging tools that help Health and Wellness Experts reinvent their inner expertise into businesses focused on helping others own their wellness, all while creating the lifestyle and passive income they themselves desire.

He empowers wellnesspreneurs to clarify the core strengths and life stories needed to correctly draw their business map to success and then program their business GPS to navigate it as directly or indirectly as they see fit.

You can learn more about Bryan, his products and services and creative strategies for leveraging online and offline growth at www.are-you-a-wellnesspreneur.com.

Connect with Bryan at:

facebook.com/bryan.harnois

ca.linkedin.com/pub/bryan-harnois/53/9a9/529

THE POWER OF A JELLY DOUGHNUT

By Ute Goldkuhle

H arvard Business School professor Howard Stevenson once defined entrepreneurship as "the pursuit of opportunity without regard to resources."

The entrepreneurial spirit has woven a path through my life. From early childhood I dreamed about being free: free to think, to express, and to act contrary to our family style of rules and order. I always sensed I did not fit.

I was a quiet, inward-drawn child but intensely restless within, curious to explore and test new things. I was not afraid to pack up, uproot, and start anew. And I did, more than once between decades, starting at age sixteen and as late as sixty-eight.

Distance was never a consideration, nor did I question why I would leave a secure life in my native country, or how I would manage in the new place. I did not have means nor skills. I just had to follow my intense urge to explore the unknown. Though each beginning was rough, the thrill of climbing a new hill to get to the other side overpowered all. My parents never understood why their third child was driven by such undefined forces, and neither did I. I was never a troublemaker, rather a helper.

I grew up during WWII. We were poor, but everybody was poor and struggling to put food on the table in our small German country town. I can still conjure the smell of freshly-baked doughnuts as I passed the bakery on my way to school. Those warm yeast jelly doughnuts coated with white powdered sugar! I baby-sat many afternoons for just one.

My bike was my friend, my freedom. I could ride wherever I wanted to, explore anything, and feel free in nature among the flowers, meadows, and fields. I loved the smells, the whistles of ripe yellowed grain, the blue cornflowers and red poppies. I was alone, away from fights with my siblings, the disapproval of my parents, and my ever-unhappy grandmother in the house.

I had to drop out of high school, closing the door on any future educational opportunities. I could become a nurse or maid; I became both. My father was embarrassed, as he had higher aspirations for his children. A nurse during that time was low on the social scale. He thought that his third child was "ein bischen dumm", meaning a little stupid.

In my early twenties, I met a handsome young man who was on his way to America. We saw each other about six times before he was off on the boat to the "Free World" he dreamed of. I could not even point to America on the map, much less identify New York, but I had to go there just as he yearned to start a new life. I had to taste once more the cheese, the magic white bread, and warm chocolate American soldiers served us school kids. I had to follow this young man. And I did, six months later. Nothing could hold me back, nothing! I had no money but I could clean houses, so I did.

Together we built a new life in America. A life we could breathe in freely with endless opportunities. We felt rewarded for our hard work. Each time I carried my newborn son up eight flights of stairs to our little railroad flat in New York, I felt like I was carrying him closer to heaven. He was our pride—born in America! And so was his little brother soon after. Life was open to them. They could become president one day, for God's sake!

Opportunities were everywhere! On Monday nights the streets became our furniture and clothing stores. A table for the kitchen, a comfy chair to nurse my boys, all for the taking! My son, now forty-seven, still has that chair. I could take free classes to learn English. My husband could start his own business with nothing and pursue his artistic passion in stained glass.

Nobody cared what school we went to, whether I had dropped out of school, what family we were born into. The doors to learn and pursue a profession were as wide open in America as they were closed in Germany during the post-WWII era.

I couldn't have envisioned reaching great professional heights in Germany and earning a doctorate degree at age fifty-six. After all, I had flunked my first test in college. My father was right, I am 'ein bischen dumm,' I thought. But the teacher would not let me quit. "You can always quit. You have not even started, and don't forget, you paid for the course!" His voice still talks to me when I feel like throwing in the towel. I hoped one day I would be able to model that teacher. And I did.

"Aren't you too old to run that marathon?" I was asked. "No, I am only sixty-two!" And I made it to the finish line, earning my jelly doughnut. Yes, a jelly doughnut is still today my secret reward after difficult struggles. Struggles like getting the last signature of a committee member to sign off my dissertation. He stalled for two semesters, and nothing was right or good enough, but I finally prevailed. I can still taste the first bite into my jelly doughnut when the battle to escape bankruptcy was over.

This is my never-ending journey, always pursuing opportunities of unknown results, or so I thought until a month ago.

"You had a heart attack—not a common one caused by a blockage but by an over-stressed, failing heart," the doctor said while I was tied to tubes and beeping monitors in the emergency room.

"A failing heart? A stressed heart? That can't be. I am a healthy person, feeling fit most of the time! I ought to know and understand hearts at risk. I have studied, researched, and devoted over 45 years of my professional life to health and wellness care! I am halfway through training for a 10K race. Sure, I have had to deal with stressful situations! But who has not?" I argued in disbelief and felt defeated.

Could this be the end soon? I wondered silently as I was overcome with fear and uncertainty. I am not finished with life yet. I have more plans and am still working on being that special grandmother I read about but never knew. Most of all, I have just begun giving back to the community for all I have received throughout the years. Is this just a dream?

When my first grandchild was born, I made a commitment to stay healthy and fit so I could have fun with him and all my future grandchildren. Even more, I wanted to inspire them to appreciate a healthy lifestyle and to explore the world.

My grandmother, the only one I knew, was not fun to be with. She seemed not to like children. She was grossly overweight and unhealthy, physically and mentally. Her life is profoundly embedded in how I approach my aging and life as a grandmother. I thank her often for showing me what NOT to do. She laid the foundation for my intentions in my grandmother role.

When little Jolena wrote in her seven-year-old spelling, "I think I have a trific gramma," or when I read a hand-crafted Valentine's Day card from my grandchildren saying, "Iron Oma We Love You!" I get a sense that my intentions are working. But I don't want to stop here.

Throughout my professional life working with older adults, I learned that life is not going well for many other aging grandmothers. They experience many health and social issues, preventing them from being that grandmother they want to be. I wished to reach out to them and make a slight difference to ease their aging life and lift their spirits.

How could I leave unfinished work behind? I thought from that hospital bed. My mind and my now-stressed heart felt so unprepared, confused, and humbled. "No, this is not the end soon," I heard an inner voice whisper. "You are just beginning!"

Was this the voice of the teacher who pulled and pushed me forward? Was it the power of the entrepreneurial spirit in the NAMS community encouraging me once more? Was it my family or my grandchildren who may want to know more of what is still hidden in my soul?

The beeping monitors and tubes have long disappeared. The work has just begun to write, to give, and to inspire fellow grandmothers and seniors to enlighten their soul.

We move through life and suddenly ask, "How did I get here?", or "how did this or that happen?" Others may ask, "How can I get there?" Here are my humble thoughts:

- Find your deeply buried dreams, nurture them, and let them shine—it's never too early and never too late.
- Trust your inherent genius, have fun showing and sharing it.
- Always, always hold true to your values despite diverting temptations; trust that they are your strongest weapons to climb and reach the life mountain.

And, don't forget, those jelly doughnuts are waiting—thousands of them. Grab them while chasing your dreams!

ABOUT THE AUTHOR

Ute Goldkuhle, DrPH enjoys life with her six grandchildren today after a rich career in public health as a nurse practitioner, teacher, and researcher. A life-long entrepreneur at heart, she finally is able to open her creative mind and build a community for grandmothers and senior women: www.FunFitandHealthyGrandma. com. It is a community to uplift, support and inform to feel healthy and well regardless of limitations or disability. She is finishing her first book: *Happy Smoothie Hour with the*

Grandchildren — Chats and Giggles over Grandma's Special Smoothies, Filled with Healthy Twists and Fun Tricks.

Connect with Ute at:

facebook.com/FunFitandHealthyGrandma

twitter.com/UteGoldkuhle1

plus.google/+UteGoldkuhle

HUMBLED BY A
BOX OF CHEERIOS

By Paul Counts

M y entire business was transformed the night my pregnant
wife and two-year-old daughter had to eat Cheerios for
dinner. Humiliated, saddened, and disgusted with how we
got to that place, I finally had the boost I needed to change my family's
future and never look back!

That day occurred in March 2009 in Oklahoma, where we then
lived. I was twenty-three, and my wife was eight months pregnant
with our second child. I had been in business for myself since junior
high school and had been selling over the Internet since 2001, when I
was sixteen. At age thirteen I was a custom apparel representative and
sold licensed collegiate apparel through my basic web sites.

This financial crisis we experienced was preventable had I listened to
my mentors and safeguarded my business.

I was driving our 2001 Mercury Cougar to the airport, over an hour
from our house. On the way the car started to act strange and make
funny noises. Then it felt like the bottom just fell out of it. I pulled off

to the side of the highway and discovered the transmission had gone out, along with a few other costly components.

We barely had two nickels to rub together, and I was flying to speak at an Internet marketing event in Atlanta. I was to speak about SEO and traffic generation. I was doing a lot of that for clients, but I wasn't billing enough; I was making my clients rich and not making myself my top-paying client. I also had some revenue coming in from my affiliate sites or blogs, but I was not capturing leads from my sites. These business issues I had were coupled with being a young parent, and you could see how it got to this point.

Back to the side of the road: I called my wife to let her know the situation. I was about twenty minutes from the airport, so it was at least an hour from our home in Stillwater, Oklahoma. My wife and two-year-old eventually got to me, but along the way my wife hit a toll road and couldn't afford to pay the toll. The kind person working that day paid the difference to get her through to me.

We did not have AAA or any other roadside assistance insurance, and we couldn't afford the tow. We had to have the car impounded until we could pay for the towing and such. We were all hungry, so on the way we stopped at a fast food restaurant. Our order was less than ten dollars, but when they tried my debit cards and credit cards they were all declined. Earlier in that day our bank had hit a negative balance, and we didn't realize it.

Dejected, we walked out of the restaurant. I was embarrassed, and my wife was visibly upset and emotional. We had a box of Cheerios in the car that we brought as a snack for our daughter, and that became supper. On the drive home I vowed that would never happen again and strategized what I would do to ensure that. That moment started a monumental shift in how I ran my business.

I want to point out that we could have asked my parents or my wife's parents for financial help. In fact, when I told this story later, they were upset I didn't say anything. We also had friends in church who would have helped, but I was too prideful then to ask. Lesson number one was to not be afraid to ask for help or admit you need it. That philosophy alone increased my business.

I changed three things in my business after this incident:

1. I decided to focus more efforts on list-building (lead generation)
2. I would make more information training products available, and
3. From that point on that I would be my highest-paying client.

Despite my years of doing business online, it took me eight years to really realize how valuable list-building was to my long-term success. I heard many of the course creators I followed talk about list-building, but I didn't take action on it or take it to heart. If I had been building a list, my income and traffic levels would have been much more consistent.

I soon realized that once you have an email list, you can easily let them know about your new offers or even let them know about relevant affiliate offers for which you can earn a commission. Until then the affiliate marketing I was doing relied on SEO and some online videos to get traffic. Though it made money, the income was like a yo-yo until I started capturing names and emails.

Instead of promoting affiliate offers on review pages, I began to offer free reports to entice people to join my email list. I would follow up with them later. Using an autoresponder such as Aweber, I am able to capture my website visitor's emails as they submit them and automatically follow up with related affiliate offers or my own offers. I am pointing traffic to a landing page, or 'squeeze page,' as they are referred to in some industries.

A squeeze page is a simple one-page website with one goal: to squeeze the visitor's information. For best results you want to minimize navigation on that page. You also want to offer a free report, free video training, or free audio to encourage them to sign up and join your list. In our industry we refer to that as an ethical bribe.

I also realized the huge power in selling more of my own information products online and pushing harder to sell a course I had already developed. There is also a great list-building component to your own information product. You can really generate a great list of buyers. Soon after this incident, I finished a product I had in the works and made a quick $5,000.

The next year, 2010, I had my first product that did over $100,000 in sales. That was when I realized the power of joint venture relationships, list-building, and product-creation all in one. That really helped keep my income at a consistent level.

Besides the newfound focus on list-building and product-creation, I also made sure I was my highest-paying client. For much of my online business career, the bulk of my income was from SEO, content creation, and website work for other clients. Even though it was rewarding and offered me the opportunity to work from home, I was still trading time for dollars. I found that it was hard to budget because paydays weren't consistent, plus I realized how much money I was making my clients. I would see their sales coming in as I tracked my efforts for them. It took me awhile to realize that I could be doing that for myself. The incident in March 2009 led me to the point where I only have one remaining client I work for. I eventually "fired" my other clients so I could make myself my top-paying client. If I do want SEO or traffic consulting clients again, I can charge a premium because I don't need their business to survive, which has increased my perceived value.

In the end I learned that with some good focus, you can overcome adversity.

ABOUT THE AUTHOR

Paul Counts is an internationally-recognized information product-creation expert who has created products for professional athletes and best-selling authors. He has created dozens of step-by-step video products that have grossed millions of dollars in sales.

An entrepreneur since selling pencils in second grade, Counts has been generating money online since 2001. He also hosted a radio show that aired in Oklahoma and two other states called the Count On Us Internet Profits.

You can get more information at www.paulcounts.com.

Connect with Paul at:

www.facebook.com/pages/paul-counts/103438693058984

twitter.com/paulcounts

www.linkedin.com/in/paulcounts

plus.google.com/116940851344964518542

CROOKS, CRIMINALS & CON-ARTISTS – THE CONSPIRACY AGAINST YOU & ME

by Brian G. Johnson

I f you've been searching for a better, more rewarding and fulfilling life, this may be the most worthwhile text you've read in a long time.

As you read this, there is a conspiracy against you and me. The conspiracy comes from our own negative thoughts as well as the naysayers around us. The crooks, criminals, and con artists conspire against your every move. Their goal is to keep you from believing that you can, in fact, have a rewarding and satisfying life.

This conspiracy has crushed the hopes and dreams of many good people. The victims forget what it's like to dream and believe. Consequently, these folks are leading lives they never planned on living — lives that lack fulfillment, inspiration, and meaningful rewards. Unwittingly, they settled for mediocrity!

85

I've been battling this conspiracy my entire life and, make no mistake, it has in the past held me back from living a rich, gratifying life. That was true until I finally confronted and then crushed those that have conspired against me. I am now opening up and sharing this with you because I hope that you'll be able to use this information to achieve what you want out of life: great relationships, solid finances, and inspirational purpose.

My Backstory

In 2003, after working as a professional chef for more than a dozen years, I submitted my two weeks' notice. I staked my claim and set out to live life my way -- calling my own shots and answering to only myself. I intended to enjoy the freedom that working for oneself brings, which is exactly what I had wanted since I was about eight years old.

It was never about driving a Ferrari or making millions. Rather, my dream was simply to live an exciting life on my own terms, to play the starring role in my own Hollywood blockbuster and to live a life of thrilling adventures. And my life has been filled with joy and pleasure ever since.

Thanks to the Internet, I generated millions of dollars in revenue over the past 12 or so years. I traveled the world, shared my story from various stages, and released three #1 best selling Amazon Kindle books. One was ranked #8 out of 164,000+ books in the Business & Money category of the Kindle store, and it actually outsold *The Wolf of Wall Street* as well as the contemporaneous Steve Jobs biography.

What is most gratifying for me, however, is that I have had the honor of mentoring many people and coaching thousands more to make good money online with the training programs I created and released over the years. Best of all, I'm just getting warmed up while continually reaching for greater heights. The future is bright, and for that I am thankful.

Helping others achieve life-changing results online is my calling, and I'm very good at it. It's the thing that gets me out of bed at 4:30 in the morning to film a video or post to my blog. I know that doing so may impact at least one person in a positive way. To be able to inspire, educate, and entertain people as they work to better themselves is the one gift I intend not to waste. I am sharing this with you not to brag but rather to set the scene and provide you with the right perspective.

You should also know that I struggle, perhaps just like you. I make one mistake after another and in the process leave a trail of screw-ups that's visible from space (or at least throughout the Internet). It's within these screw-ups that the internal conspiracy goes to work, as it creeps into the inner workings of my mind and says I'm not good enough, I'm not smart enough, people are not interested, everyone will laugh at me. These are the negative thoughts that fill my brain and cloud my judgment.

It's not just fear and self-doubt that are in on the conspiracy, though. Many people see the glass as half full; they have given up on their own dreams and ambitions and are bent on bringing others down as well.

These Negative Nellies are another part of the conspiracy against me and often will do their best to crush my dreams by filling my head with more negativity. Their negativity feeds back into my mind, and the psychological warfare begins all over again. However, I won't let all that affect me as I push past the fear, self-doubt, and limiting beliefs.

Success is not found in a piece of software, a powerful WordPress plugin, or a theme pack. Success cannot be obtained by hiring a mentor, a coach, or a "business in a box" system that nearly guarantees results. Rather, success is often found when one believes that it is possible and has faith that the desired results can be achieved.

> *"Whether you think you can or think that you can't—you're right."*
> **—Henry Ford**

Over the years, I have taken countless risks and made many mistakes. It was scary, and I worried a lot. I knew it was necessary to push past my fears, though, and I never gave in to them. I would never let that con artist in my head—or anyone else, for that matter—prevent me from taking action, moving forward, and being the best Brian G. Johnson I can be. I am willing to take huge chances in order to reach my goals. I am ready to put myself out there in order to do what is needed to get the results I seek. Today, I stake my claim, and there is nobody who can slow my progress!

My profession as an Internet marketer is based on publishing content, but it's interesting to note that I actually have the grammar and spelling skills of a eighth grader. On Facebook I constantly post amazingly fun and exciting graphics that could be legendary if not for the fact that they contain jarring spelling and/or grammar mistakes. As they should, my friends call me out on these mistakes, and I cringe while wondering what the world thinks of me.

Men and women of wisdom say that magic happens when life is lived outside of comfort zones, when we face our fears while doing what's needed in order to achieve positive results. Fear and the negativity conspiracy that we all face has never stopped me from pressing on and taking chances. Therefore, I've continued to grow in business and in my personal life, and the rewards have been sweet. I surround myself with positive peers, mentors, and coaches who inspire me to be my best.

If you struggle to find energy and courage, look for others who are filled with these qualities and absorb the positive vibes they radiate. The power of a good coach or an encouraging mentor should never be underestimated. Can you imagine what the Karate Kid would have done without Mr. Miyagi? Or what might have become of the Italian Stallion (Rocky Balboa) without the help, guidance, and mentoring of his trainer, Mickey? Imagine Star Wars with no Yoda! I shudder to think what might have happened to Luke Skywalker as he faced the evil Darth Vader.

It is powerful to have a mentor who believes in you and your dreams. Alternatively, a network of people who tell you it's not possible or that you're foolish to try will have a devastating impact on your outlook and mental state. Hanging around those who tell you you're not smart enough or not good enough is highly toxic.

Unfortunately, there are many people who are programmed with negativity, and they know no other way. Consequently, they tend to put down all others who dare to dream by telling them that it's not possible, it's a waste of time, it's stupid to try, it's not good enough. Make no mistake, if you hear "you're stupid" enough times, chances are you will start to believe it. Then you chalk one up to the crooks, the con artists, and the conspiracy to bring you down!

We all face this negativity at some point in our lives. I have experienced it several times, and I can tell you with certainty that the more time I spent with these crooks and criminals, the more I worried. And the more I worried, the harder it became to face my fears. In fact, such negative programming nearly caused me to bail on some important dreams.

Perhaps you've heard the following quote from Jim Rohn: "You are the average of the five people you spend the most time with."

I fully believe this to be true. When I was younger I participated in many sports and always trained with those who were smarter, faster, and better than me. This raised my game, and today I am very selective about who to accept into my network of personal and business associates. Only those who have a positive outlook are welcome. I simply cannot afford to be surrounded by negative energy or to be influenced by naysayers who attempt to derail the direction I am heading, to negatively impact what I am doing, and to criticize the life I live. Staying positive is important, but so is being proactive in taking the needed action that will lead to success.

I encourage you to face your fears and never let them stop you from doing the things you want or need to do. Perhaps you want to tell someone you love them, or you want to build your dream house near the ocean or in the mountains. Maybe your dream is like mine and that is to work for yourself, call the shots, and live your life as an entrepreneur.

You can do anything you set your mind to because anything is possible. It begins with a dream and a defined goal. Then it requires taking action to end up where you want to be.

Over the years I have leveraged a success ritual that has had a massive impact on my life. "Be clear and exact about what you truly want. Stake your claim; announce that it will be yours. Fully commit to having it and do what is needed in order to make it happen. Believe that it is possible, because it is."

The success ritual is incredibly powerful, as it sets your mind in motion in order to solve a problem and help you to fulfill your dreams and reach your goals. It begins with being clear on what you want and how you intend to achieve it. Too many individuals dream about success but do not create a plan to help them achieve it. It's no wonder they aimlessly drift through life even as they wonder what might have been.

Of course, a dream alone is simply not enough to generate tangible results. You must be willing to grab the bull by the horns and take massive action to live up to your dreams and aspirations. Don't worry! You don't have to go it alone. Find others who are doing what you want to do, study their movements, and duplicate their efforts. If you want massive results, you must be prepared to take massive action.

ABOUT THE AUTHOR

Brian G. Johnson is a serial entrepreneur, engaging speaker, product creator, #1 bestselling author, nurturing mentor and passionate poodle wrangler. Since 2008 Brian has coached tens of thousands of wealth seekers, many of whom are successfully generating life-changing income.

Brian's high energy and zest for life translate well into his coaching programs, where he breaks down the most important elements characteristic to many profitable online businesses — traffic and conversions. His formulas are simple, his rituals are effective and his techniques are rather easy to follow.

Learn more about Brian and his powerful Internet marketing strategies at:

MarketingEasyStreet.com
facebook.com/marketingeasystreet
YouTube.com/user/marketingeasyst
plus.google.com/u/0/+BrianGJohnson-MarketingEasySt
twitter.com/marketingeasystreet

WIN WITH WHAT YOU BRING TO THE TRACK

By Gary Huff

M any adventures and lessons growing up eventually shape and form our lives. Some of my most distinct childhood memories were the times I spent with my dad at the drag races. My dad was involved with drag racing even before I was born, and it became a natural place for us to spend time together. As an adult, I now look back on those times and find that they mattered a lot. Those trips created important life lessons: seeing the dragsters speed down the track, spending time with my dad, and getting a behind-the-scenes look at a drag race.

Professional Spectator

Drag racing is really about two cars and drivers pitted against each other to see who can get to the end of the track the fastest. As a spectator, you may watch the action but may not see the details. Drag racing begins with qualifying rounds, and the drivers with the top times move on to the final day of eliminations. For the first couple days, qualifying is about racing the clock. The real fun comes during the final day of elimination, when the winner is decided. As the two dragsters approach the starting line, they are no longer competing against the clock; they're racing only each other. What matters is who crosses the finish line first.

When my dad and I started going to the track, I was too little to understand the mechanics of dragsters. I was simply able to appreciate fast cars speeding down a track. A typical spectator may be watching the race from that perspective. But my dad, who's been in drag racing his whole life, helped me become a professional spectator.

The term professional spectator can apply to any event, your business, or your family. A professional spectator is someone who doesn't merely watch the event unfold but understands the mechanics behind the scenes. As a Professional Drag Race Spectator, I was able to appreciate the many aspects of preparation and understand why things happened on the track. For example, dragsters will occasionally do a burn-out and smoke their tires. It's a very spectacular thing to see. From a typical spectator standpoint, it's just part of the entertainment. But from the professional spectator perspective, I understand that the drivers are really heating the tire rubber to better grip the track. That grip makes the difference between a winning run and not getting down the track.

There are countless other ways to observe as professional spectators in the drag racing world and in all parts of our lives. At a business engagement, with friends, or with family, I often take the professional spectator perspective to not just hear what people are saying but to understand the meaning behind the event and discussion.

Win With What You Bring To The Track

My dad and I would visit the track several times a year as I was growing up. Nowadays, times at the track with my dad are far and few between. The time spent with my dad was very important. I learned Dad's thoughts and insights that he might not have discussed elsewhere.

One of Dad's great insights from the track has helped me in my life and my business. We were discussing how some drag racing teams continually win more races than others. I asked, "What about those teams consistently makes them winners?" Dad answered, "In drag racing, like so many things in life, you have to be able to win with what you bring to the track."

When I heard it the first time, I remember thinking, Okay, they've brought the car, parts, engine, and tires, and won with that. But later in life I realized his insight instructs how we handle our tasks, our job, and the challenges ahead of us. Consistently winning teams didn't necessarily have a better engine, tires, or driver (though all do matter). The key was, on that particular weekend, on that particular track, they were able to pull together the right combination of the right pieces and win with what they brought to the track that day. I take that lesson from dad and try to use it throughout my life. I will always want more skills, time, or tools, but I can still win with what I have with me right now.

The Crew Chief

At the racetrack there are three areas: the spectator area, the race track, and the pits. As a little kid, the pits were the exciting place to be. It looked like chaos—cars moving in and out, people walking around, people watching, mechanics and pit crews working on cars. Then cars would test fire their engines. One of the big excitements in the pits is to witness a top fuel dragster firing up its engine just fifteen feet away. You smell the nitro burning and hear the loud noise. It's hard to explain; you have to experience it for yourself.

I operate similar to the pit area. A lot of work happens behind the scenes so the spectators can see their favorite dragsters speed down the track. That behind-the-scenes work really inspires and interests me. A drag race team will finish a pass down the track, bring the car back to their pit area, and almost completely dismantle and rebuild the engine from the bottom up for the next race. Modern-day drag racing is so competitive that parts in the engine are meant to last just one trip down the track. Parts are pulled and analyzed. The level of computer technology involved in a dragster traveling a quarter-mile down a track is phenomenal.

The role of crew chief really resonates with me. Specialists on the drag race team work on the engine, the clutch, and so much more. Every aspect of the dragster requires a specialist in that particular area. The crew chief may be well-experienced in many of those areas, but his role is to unite his team of diverse and critical experts into a focused effort, to prepare the dragster, and then hand it over to the driver to get a win.

The crew chief reflects what I try to accomplish in my business and my family life. Like a crew chief, you must identify the expertise and talent needed in the team, focusing those skills in the right area at the right time. You must be sure the task is 100% ready, and then release control of it with the confidence that you've provided the driver the tools and ability to get to the finish line faster than the guy in the next car.

Being a crew chief involves understanding people, understanding processes, and even more important, understanding that you can't do it all yourself. Someone else ultimately gets in that car and drives it down the track. I take that approach in my work as an operations and project manager, to help the team effectively accomplish its goals, to further utilize and develop the tools and capabilities they bring with them, and then let the right person drive it to the finish.

ABOUT THE AUTHOR

 Gary Huff is known as the Overwhelm Escape Artist and has held increased leadership responsibility in operations, industrial engineering, quality, logistics, marketing, and project management in several diverse departments and businesses. Gary possesses a unique blend of interpersonal skills, operational experience, project management expertise, and effective communication skills. Gary has a proven track record in leading teams in developing superior processes and products that deliver on customer needs and impact the overall company operations.

Gary is a PMI® Certified Project Management Professional (PMP®) with 30+ years expertise with a $70B Transportation and Logistics

Company. Gary provides strategy, business model development, operations improvement, and development programs through coaching and consulting of individual entrepreneurs, small to medium businesses, and large corporate clients across the world. Over the past couple years, Gary has launched twelve Mentoring groups and 17 Mastermind groups with over 450 participants.

Learn more about Gary at overwhelmescapeartist.com/

Connect with Gary at:

www.facebook.com/OverwhelmEscapeArtist

twitter.com/GaryHuff

www.linkedin.com/profile/view?id=130477310

CREATING A REAL BUSINESS

By Jama St. John

W hat do you want to be when you grow up? We've all heard that question.

As far back as I can remember, I wanted to be a secretary. When I was in fourth grade, my mom gave me an old manual typewriter—the kind that required you beat on the keys for the letters to be imprinted on the paper. After I became pretty good at the hunt-and-peck method, my mom taught me to type the correct way. She showed me where to put my fingers and what finger pushed what key. I loved to type and spent hours retyping magazine articles. Eventually, I upgraded to a portable electric typewriter.

By the time I got to high school typing class, I was rockin' it! I still wanted to be a secretary, and I still loved typing!

I went to business college and worked as a legal secretary and administrative assistant for ten years. In 1996, I started my own business. I didn't know what I was getting into! The information available now was not readily available back then. My parents were small business owners, so I guess the entrepreneurial bug was inevitable, but I knew very little about how to run a business. I didn't even go to the library for books on how to start and run a business. I just winged it! It wasn't the wisest move I've ever made.

I knew enough of the basics to get started, though, and I was good at doing the work. I started with a combination of in-office work and transcription services, which I was able to do from home. The best part was that I could be at home with my kids, and I didn't have to be at work at 8:00 every morning. (I am not a morning person.)

I always enjoyed my business, and it has gone through several transformations over the past 18 years. Actually, even though I called it a business, it really wasn't one until just a few years ago. I had a hobby, not a plan. I ran my "business" by the seat of my pants.

I was a solo Virtual Assistant, and I loved being behind the scenes and making things happen for my clients. I prefer to stay behind the scenes because I'm an introvert, on the shy side, and I don't comfortably meet new people. If someone had told me in 1996 that I would need to attend networking events and talk to people I didn't know, I might never have started my business.

My kids were extroverts, and I still wonder where they got it from. My son wrote and played music, produced his own CD, and played at clubs in Orlando, Florida, when he was twenty. I was in awe. I wondered how could he get up in front of all of those people and play music that he wrote. My daughter is also outgoing and will talk to anybody. She continues to amaze me and attends networking events with me when she can. She's awesome at talking with people. Where do they get it? Certainly not from me!

For years, I did what I had to, but sometimes I was so nervous just before meeting new people that I would want to throw up. Have you ever been there?

In late 2009, I decided it was time to get serious and create a real business—not just a hobby that was paying the bills, or a job I'd created for myself that left me with no free time. I wanted a business that more than paid the bills and allowed me to spend time with my son in Florida and my daughter who would soon be moving out of our Georgia house. But then, in March 2010, something totally unimaginable happened.

My twenty-one-year old son was struck and killed by an automobile.

I remember that weekend like it was yesterday, yet it seems so long ago. I thought about calling him that evening but didn't. After all, it was a Saturday night and if he wasn't working, he was probably hanging out with friends. This was about an hour before the accident.

At 8:30 Sunday morning, the deputy sheriff was at our door. I wondered, What has my daughter done? He asked if I had a son Stefan, who lived in Orlando, and then I thought, Oh, what has Stefan done? The sheriff continued, "There has been an accident, and he's been killed." My knees buckled as I started to fall to the ground.

How do you recover from that?

Four years later, it's still a day-by-day process. There are still times when those "what if" thoughts go through my mind: What if I had called that night? What if I had convinced him to move to Georgia? Then I remember the Serenity Prayer: God, grant me the serenity to accept the things I cannot change, the courage to change the things I can, and the wisdom to know the difference.

There is not a day that goes by that I don't think of him. Some days are much harder than others. If there is anything good to have come out of it, it's that my daughter and I now have a much closer relationship. You really do have to find the gem in the pile of rubble to get through an experience like that.

Once I picked myself up off the floor and found my new normal, I went back to my business. Have you ever been so busy that your own business needs get put on the back burner? You work in your business instead of on it? I've been there, done that. I finally took my own advice and hired a business coach and a virtual assistant. Of course, my VA is my daughter, who works with me along with several clients of her own. That makes a mama proud! I also hired an online business manager and a virtual chief financial officer. You must have the right people in place to help you with your business.

I'm still an introvert, but I have learned to put my big girl boots on and step it up. I attend networking events and even travel out of state to events where I don't know anyone (oh my!). I lead online and in-person group training on Infusionsoft. The funny thing is, the more you do something, the easier it gets. But if you don't do it again for a long time, it gets hard again. I make sure I regularly attend events, and I started a weekly podcast to keep me active online and talking to people.

At Strategic Virtual Solutions, we help clients implement their online and offline marketing strategies. Through the years, we've watched trends change and expand, and our talents change with those trends. We enjoy the behind-the-scenes action. We're introverts! But as the owner of this multi-virtual assistant company, I have to remind myself that I can't just be the behind-the-scenes implementer. I must also be out there talking with people.

Remember you can do whatever you want to do no matter what you perceive your limitations to be and whatever life challenges come your way. You really can do it.

ABOUT THE AUTHOR

Jama St. John is the President of Strategic Virtual Solutions ("SVS"), which offers consulting, implementation and virtual assistant services for busy entrepreneurs. SVS provides Infusionsoft support from installation to training and ongoing maintenance, as well as manages product launches, internet marketing, social media, telesummit/virtual events, and website design for entrepreneurs, including business coaches, speakers, and authors. Jama produces a weekly podcast where she interviews successful entrepreneurs. She is also the author of Marketing for Small Businesses: Creating an Amazing Referral Program. For more information, please visit www.StrategicVirtualSolutions.net.

Connect with Jama at:

facebook.com/strategicvirtualsolutions

twitter.com/strategicvs

www.linkedin.com/in/jamastjohn

plus.google.com/u/0/+JamaStJohn

LIFE TO THE THIRD DEGREE

By Jeanne Kolenda

I am the oldest of a "tribe" of six kids. We are all so different you couldn't pick us out of a lineup as being related. There are now fifty-two of us in the family—siblings, spouses, children, and grandchildren. We have to rent a place to have a family dinner. My parents were madly in love for forty-two years until my father died suddenly of a heart attack in 1989. Mom, at age eighty-seven, still kisses his picture every morning and evening. I realize now we were poor, but I didn't notice then because life was so full of rich things—books, music, art, travel. Daddy was a Pentecostal preacher and a fine architect and builder. Every time a church needed a new building, they were quite sure God was calling my father to assist. More often than not, he went, I think out of the sheer joy of adventure. I attended at least twelve schools in as many years. I never considered all the moving as abnormal, and my natural people skills made it easy to adapt.

I was a brainiac and graduated high school at sixteen. Off to college I went, hardly ready emotionally or socially. I quickly went down in an inglorious blaze of my own making. Kicked out of school for bad behavior (to put it mildly), I returned home, became pregnant, and got married, in that order. My son was born four days before my 18th birthday. A beautiful daughter came into my life when I was twenty. I had a ready-made job—raising my children.

I did return to college when they started school, graduating with degrees in English, Math, and Biology (don't ask!). This set the stage for our family to join the pioneers of the home school movement a few years later. Remember, this was over thirty years ago, and some of us were actually arrested for "contributing to the delinquency of a minor by way of truancy." People who now choose home education have no idea the price that was paid for this simple freedom to decide how to best educate our children.

My daddy was a brilliant man and loved learning; he passed that on to me. It wasn't enough to study Scripture; he had to read it in Hebrew and Greek to catch all the nuances. He was a numerologist concerning the ancient writings, and numbers have always had meaning to me. I found many things in life come in groups of three. The Trinity, for starters (Father, Son, Holy Spirit). Then I realized there is a Trinity of almost everything: Primary colors (red, blue, yellow), Time (past, present, future), Matter (liquid, solid, gas), the Nature of Man (body, soul, and spirit), Dimensions (height, width, depth), Trees (root, trunk, branches), even an egg (shell, yolk, white).

Why am I telling you this? Because I have a trinity that guides everything I do. I call it the C^3 Syndrome. Everything I do is guided by a word that begins with C—Communicate, Connect, Collaborate. Thus, the title for this chapter is "Life to the Third Degree."

It all started to come together for me in 1977, though not very clearly at first. There I was, with two children born before I was twenty-one, and they were then six and eight. We were at Lake Lure, North Carolina, and while the children attended a church-sponsored event, I took my Bible, my notebook, and a pen down to a dock on the lake.

I've always been drawn to the epic stories in the Old Testament. I was on a mission to discover what was real and to be embraced, and what was man-made and could be tossed aside. I was looking closely at the prophets Ezra and Nehemiah, who rebuilt the ancient walls of their city. It's a great study in leadership and humility, and an example of how individuals can have a significant impact on history. These men built something of importance and beauty out of charred remnants of a rubbish heap.

Now, consider where I was in life—a young wife and mother with two small children, no college education, and no career goals. (My kids were my career, and I chose well, by the way.) According to everyone else's perceptions, I had made quite a mess of my life so far, with many bad decisions. But that day on the dock of Lake Lure, I caught a glimpse of what God had planned for my life—and it was in a group of three! Ezra 7:10 became my life verse, though it was decades before it all came to pass. Here's what I saw: the Scripture says Ezra set out to 1) study, 2) practice what he learned, and 3) teach others. Boom! I had my marching orders. I would study, learn to implement, and one day teach others. I realized that something important and meaningful could come of my "rubbish heap."

It has happened just like that. And by doing things in this order, I am naturally saved from being a fake. No "fake it till you make it" for me. Even today, when I'm planning what product to create or offer to my growing list of followers in my Internet marketing business, I can't and won't offer something I haven't tried and found to be helpful and useful. I may not get as rich as other marketers, but I won't have to worry about my reputation.

In 1989, there came another set of three: Death, Defeat, and Divorce. My father died suddenly and was buried on the day my divorce was finalized, after a twenty-year marriage. I felt defeated because I didn't believe in divorce. I still don't, and I think it's like trying to unscramble eggs. That year, too, brought the beginning of empty nest syndrome as my firstborn left for college in a distant state. I survived, and it wasn't long before I met and married Leon, the love of my life. We've now been together twenty-five years, and with God's grace and mercy, we have a beautiful and healthy marriage for which we are very grateful. My children are now forty-five and forty-two, and they are my dearest friends on earth. Many parents would pay to have the kind of kids I have. Leon has two children, and we have six grandchildren.

When Leon and I married, he taught me that everything I had done to raise healthy children and manage a home would translate well into the business world. Being an entrepreneur, he taught me about business: how to spot an opportunity and make it happen. My first opportunity came when we moved from Seattle to Myrtle Beach. Unbelievably, there was no voicemail service, not even with the phone companies. We searched and found a telephony switch, purchased it, and set up a telecommunications business. That business is still going strong after twenty years, even though the phone companies rolled out their versions soon after we opened. It is the financial base for everything else I want to do.

With my communication skills and my ability to connect in a new community, I soon became a sought-after resource for all things digital. That led to a partnership with my friend Sue White. We opened Business Training Team in 2010, offering free weekly webinars to members of the Chambers of Commerce in our area. We taught businesses how to develop online visibility with the rise of the Internet and Google. Even though our training was free, there were many local business owners who raised their hands, so to speak, to ask for help. Thus, our Internet marketing firm was born and is still a thriving and exciting business.

As Sue and I reached out for help, seeking mentors and wanting to learn more about offline marketing, we found just the right people, and they began to see the uniqueness and success of our free webinar approach with the Chambers and other non-profits. We were assisted in creating a training course for other marketers—Success With Webinars—that became a smash hit. We have continued to create products for other marketers and have recently collaborated with Brian Anderson and Syd Michael on a membership site totally dedicated to helping other marketers—LocalTrainingAcademy.com. I have never had more fun, and I'm so excited to see what's around the corner, as I continue to Communicate, Connect, and Collaborate while creating content (two more C words!)

ABOUT THE AUTHOR

Jeanne Kolenda is married to Leon Kolenda and has lived in Myrtle Beach, SC for almost twenty-five years. She is a "serial" entrepreneur, owning a telecommunications business - In Touch Solutions; a marketing firm, Business Training Team, with partner, Sue White, and is a partner with Brian Anderson and Syd Michael in www.LocalTrainingAcademy.com, a membership site dedicated to helping local marketers worldwide.

She is a mother of four and grandmother of six. She loves to ride her BMW motorcycle, and tries to knit a little every day. Traveling with Leon in their RV and still being able to work is a dream come true.

Connect with Jeanne at:

facebook.com/JeanneKolenda

twitter.com/jeannekolenda

www.linkedin.com/in/jeannekolenda

JeanneKolenda.com

I WISH I COULD TAKE THE CREDIT

By Jeff Hunt

A student office assistant pulled me out of high school geometry class to see the principal. This wasn't my first walk down that long hall to his office, but this time I was stumped. I couldn't figure out what I had done or how he had found out about it.

I arrived at the office to see a host of smiling faces. "Congratulations!" they said. "You've won a new ten-speed bike." I was confused. "Uh, okay, how did I do that?" I later learned that a woman from church who I barely knew was aware that I needed a bicycle to get to school. She had purchased a raffle ticket and put my name on it.

That wasn't the only time I experienced the Lord's blessing through other people. In college my Grandma Hunt called to say, "Mr. and Mrs. Whitaker have sent you another check." I had never had a conversation with the Whitakers except to say thanks for the $2,000 they sent each fall. My grandma's only explanation for their generosity was, "They just want to bless you, Son."

After school, I landed a job with a defense contractor that took me to Kuwait to create systems for their Air Force. When Saddam Hussein invaded, the systems we had worked several years to build were carted off to Baghdad. I got out before the invasion, but my boss hung around to help my co-workers escape. He was captured by the Iraqis, and while I'm hopeful that he was one of the foreign hostages released, I haven't heard from him again.

Years later, by the grace of God, I worked my way up the ranks of middle management in IBM. I loved the job, and at age thirty-eight, with a lot of help along the way, I had accomplished all my career goals. But something was missing.

Despite my wayward tendencies, God had blessed and watched over me my whole life. I wanted to share that blessing, the peace and assurance I had found, with people who had absolutely no access to that message. That compulsion to take a risk and share hope led me, my wife, and our four little kids to sell everything we owned and move to a small city in a far-away Muslim country.

I was sitting on an airplane in an aisle seat when a flight attendant approached me and put something in my hand. He said he had been talking to my nine-year-old daughter in the back of the plane and was touched when he heard where we were going and what we would do there. After he walked away I opened my hand to find six twenty-dollar bills.

It was illegal to be a missionary in that country, so I opened a real estate business. Eighty-seven percent of the homes in my database did not have indoor bathrooms. Homebuyers had a very unique set of questions: "How strong is the electricity?" "How big is the water tank?" "How often does the water come each week?" "Is the house near a cemetery?" I was once showing a house when a rat the size of a rabbit strolled by. I was afraid even to shoo the thing away.

Making a buck in a Third World country wasn't easy, especially if you have qualms about greasing palms. But we weren't there for business. We were there to show God's love.

College students found us. Our home became a refuge for them. In our meetings they could learn practical and eternal life strategies. They could be themselves and express their opinions. Girls and boys could talk to each other without condemnation. They could play crazy games that would never be acceptable in their own homes and universities. They were exposed to ideas that challenged the worldview forged in their culture. They developed skills that allowed them to land jobs, get accepted into programs, and travel to other countries. They could share the fears, dreams, and realities of their lives with us because they knew that we loved and cared about them. Some of their lives were changed for eternity, many others for a mere lifetime.

Although our work with students was informal by design, it certainly wasn't invisible. In the West behavior is guided by laws and an internal sense of right and wrong. In the East behavior is much more influenced by notions of honor and by gossip. The gossip is fueled by everyone carefully watching what everyone else does and reporting on it. Students showing up in droves on our doorstep, multiple times per day, certainly gave the city something to talk about.

Student-led revolutions in nearby countries did not go unnoticed by leaders in our country. Social media, specifically Facebook, was the technology that enabled their messages to spread and escalate. Facebook was the venue of choice for my students, too. Girls and guys couldn't fraternize on the streets together but they could and did spend hours together on Facebook every evening. They weren't looking for a platform for insurgency; they just wanted a safe place to hang out. I wanted to be part of their lives, so I hung out there, too.

The mayor of our city did not like Facebook, did not like foreigners, and did not like us. He was an appointee of the president of the country, with no allegiance to anyone except himself and the ruling political party. The secret police, universities, telecommunication companies, post offices, and almost all other organizations were under his control. Universities began to warn students from associating with us. Police started intimidating students and harassing us. The campaign culminated with a press conference in which the mayor named us as public enemies and vowed to shut us down.

We started getting regular, unfriendly visits from the police. Innocent students were held for interrogation simply because they had visited our home. After seven years of ministry, a house full of kids who had now grown up, and a feeling of having done what we came to do, it was time to say goodbye to hundreds of Muslim friends we had grown to love.

Back in the USA, I contemplated documenting the years in a crazy country on my resume and returning to an executive role in a corporate company. It wasn't tempting. I had grown to love the flexibility of working for myself. However, I had a family to support, two kids entering college, and a life to rebuild. It wasn't going to be cheap and we needed an income stream quickly, so I prayed and turned to the Internet.

The strategy I adopted was to buy existing websites that were already earning money every month. This was much faster and easier than starting at square one with no customers, no product, no website, and no sales. I soon found that the return on website investments is much higher than that of traditional investments. I could often get my money back in six months to a year. The strategy worked, and I've never looked back. Within four months our monthly income stream was fully supporting the family.

My buddies still in the corporate world want in on the action when they hear what I do. My websites don't require much time to operate, so I'm able to spend time on projects I really enjoy, like working on my courses and books on website investing and teaching other people how to leapfrog the masses and start making a living on the Internet quickly. I now own hundreds of income-generating websites and actively teach others how they can do the same.

I wish I could take credit for all that has happened but as James 1:17 says, "Every good and perfect gift is from above." I've long been on the receiving end of all things "good and perfect."

ABOUT THE AUTHOR

 Jeff Hunt created Heck Yeah, LLC to answer the question, "Can you make money online?" Heck Yeah you can do it! Jeff is the owner of over 300 income producing websites. He is the author of the upcoming book, *Buying a Website Business*. He speaks, teaches and coaches and is always on the lookout for the next big deal. Find out how you can get into the internet game the fast way at www.Website-Investors.com.

www.HeckYeah.org
www.Website-Investors.com
linkedin.com/in/jeffhunt11
twitter.com/Heckyeahorg

GETTING UP AFTER LIFE KNOCKS YOU DOWN

by Marcia Ming

E ven the most successful people lose their jobs, get divorced, or face serious illness, but those who come out on the other side have performed the art of reinvention. How you react to life's challenges defines who you are and determines where you end up. But getting up again is not always easy, and sometimes it seems impossible.

As a baby boomer, I'm a veteran of getting up after a life beat-down. I've been through a divorce, job loss, and a twenty-year fight with a debilitating illness—Rheumatoid Arthritis (RA).

Millions of Americans have lost their jobs, had their 401ks decimated, or lost homes to foreclosure. Some people who worked years to build businesses had to close them during the Great Recession. This kind of devastation can be crippling and can turn strong individuals into victims.

Have you ever wondered why some people bounce back while others languish for years? Successful people are able to get up again because they have developed coping skills for dealing with life's challenges.

This "Getting Up" chapter title is inspired by one of life's challenges that left me feeling as if I had been knocked to the ground and crushed. The day my supervisor and her boss informed me that my job had been eliminated, I felt like a deer caught in headlights. It took almost two years for me to really recover. But it was a classic case of a negative event with a silver lining.

Even after ten years, my RA was still being misdiagnosed. My job as a trainer required me to stand for hours. I couldn't do the work well, but I forced myself to continue because my daughter was still in college. I had to pay the bills. Losing my job forced me to make hard decisions that ultimately made my life better. I moved to another state, where I found a wonderful doctor who helped stabilize my health. Today, some people envy my lifestyle because I work from home and set my own hours, but RA is very taxing so it's important for me to be able to rest when I feel fatigued. And, while I have multiple bosses now—my clients—I can decide with whom I wish to work.

During my journey to reinvent myself after being laid off, I observed a number of people who were trapped in their setbacks. These individuals seemed to just give up—turning into complainers instead of trying to recover from their troubles. Watching them descend into permanent despair, I learned a valuable lesson. With the wrong mindset, it can be almost impossible to recover.

You need to surround yourself with positive people and keep your thoughts positive. A friend says that whenever she starts to feel too old, too fat, or too edgy, she remembers quickly to get all of that negative self-talk out of her head. Learning to control your thoughts is one of the most important skills you must develop to wage a comeback.

You can't avoid challenges, but you can certainly prepare yourself with a toolkit. Here are six simple things you can do immediately to begin to bounce back:

1. Control your stress through exercise. Instead of a rigid routine, you might try listening to your favorite music while dancing.

2. Rather than sit in a dark room, consider going for a walk to break up negative thought patterns.

3. Take a few deep breaths to bring you back to the present.

4. Sit down and write about what you are feeling. Often when I start writing, I feel dark and sad, but by the time I finish, my mood has improved significantly. It's as if I have emptied all of those dark feelings onto the page.

5. Reach out to someone you trust to vent.

6. Join an online affinity group of people dealing with similar problems.

If these activities don't work for you, find your own. The key is to develop ways to restore a positive outlook.

I also believe it is critical to face your feelings and take responsibility for your life's direction. When my marriage failed about twenty years ago, I felt very blue. I found someone to talk with who helped me focus—not on my failed marriage, but on how I would create the best life possible for my child and myself. By changing my focus, I was able to succeed at divorce in a way that I hadn't expected. Today my daughter enjoys a great relationship with her dad. She also got a wonderful education and grew into successful adult. I have become someone my friends and others turn to when they are facing their own setbacks.

After you recover from the emotional drama, it's important to assess where you are and develop a plan to move forward. Whatever your setback, you need to visualize your next steps so you can begin to move toward them. If you have lost your job, for example, see yourself finding a new one or starting a home business. Use your visual image to guide the goals you set. Break those goals into smaller tasks and objectives with time limits. Achieving small goals will help you rebuild your confidence and give you the staying power to pursue larger ones.

In this world of rapid change and innovation, it is essential to continue learning. Never let your skills stagnate. One of the most important steps I took while still working was to enroll in courses in web design and e-learning. As a journalist in the 1980s, I wrote a lot about industries that declined as technology took hold. You must be prepared for change. Everyone needs a Plan B to weather the twists and turns of an uncertain economy. This is especially important as you age.

A number of years ago, I met a young woman with a PhD who quit her job before finding a new one or deciding on a different path because she simply hated what she was doing. Together we created a support group for women facing similar challenges. At our first meeting, I mentioned that technical writers were in high demand with commensurate salaries. The woman listened attentively and took a technical writing job at a small company where she could learn the ropes. She was later able to get a position as a medical writer at a major pharmaceutical company. Today she loves what she does and earns a healthy six-figure income.

As you plan for the future, try to hedge your bets by developing multiple income streams. Even if you take a new job, consider starting a part-time business on the side. With the Internet you may be able to start a business that doesn't conflict with your job—something you will enjoy so much it feels like a hobby.

Remember that bouncing back after a setback doesn't happen overnight. Take it one day at a time and stay positive. Believing you can do it is half the battle, and before you know it, you'll find yourself smiling and enjoying the journey.

ABOUT THE AUTHOR

Marcia Ming is owner of Ming Communications, a marketing and communications consulting firm. A former business reporter, Marcia has more than thirty years experience as a communicator, consultant and trainer. In recent years she has concentrated on internet marketing strategies to grow businesses and non-profit organizations both on and offline. She currently is working on a book to inspire minorities and baby boomers to continue to reach for their dreams despite setbacks.

She created and runs several websites including Savvy Marketing Secrets (www.savvymarketingsecrets.com) which provides marketing information for small and home based businesses.

Connect with Marcia at:

facebook.com/savvymarketingonline

twitter.com/marciaming

www.linkedin.com/profile/view?id=32997728

www.google.com/+MarciaMing

LIVING TO DANCE

By Jocelyn Chouinard

One day I found myself at the helm of no fewer than ten major projects: putting together Canada's first International Egyptian Dance Festival, finalizing details for my annual tour to Turkey, planning my next teaching tour in Europe, choreographing and rehearsing with my Egyptian Dance Ensemble, and so much more. I had to do all this before running out the door to teach Flamenco classes!

In the middle of this whirlwind of activity, which was a typical, count-down-the-minutes-to-the-next-thing kind of day, I stopped, took a big, slow, and deep breath, and asked myself, "How in the world did I get here, doing all of this? What is my plan? Why am I doing all of these time-consuming and crazy but really fun and challenging things?" Suddenly I saw my mom in front of me, her arms folded and eyes directed toward the heavens, saying to me again, "Oh dear, what in the world are we ever going to do with you, since you are neither useful nor decorative?"

Images of my life flashed by—theater, dance, music, massage therapy—traveling around the world and back again many times. Above all I remember being five years old, prancing around the living room, dancing my heart out to Swan Lake. When the summer weather arrived, I gathered up all the neighborhood kids and put on shows: circuses, plays, and my creative interpretation of Ed Sullivan (my favorite). I was producer, artistic director, MC, and star and could count on a guaranteed audience of moms to cheer and applaud. On the occasional day when I couldn't round up enough kids to do a show, I set up big cardboard boxes and stools and taught them school, even though I had no idea what school was or what happened there.

Then came my first summer at camp, where I earned the distinguished title of Kid With The Most Demerit Points In Camp History, for silly things like selling dead fish to parents for $1 on visitors day and regularly wandering off to explore instead of doing my chores. One day at lunch I had an idea. I went to each table and whispered, "Meet by the big tree at 12:15." I was thrilled to step outside and see the majority of the campers gathered in a circle, so I jumped into the center of the crowd and did cartwheels and handstands. Although I got a healthy round of applause, I was also awarded yet more demerits!

By revisiting these memories from the past, I realized that I was simply doing the same activities I had always done. I was born to do these things and knew that I was born to do them from the ripe old age of five: dance, create, perform, organize, promote, produce, massage, and teach.

Then school changed everything. Between the ages of six and seventeen, I side-tracked myself with other options: being a saint, or at least a nun (until I found out what that meant), a mathematician, a hippie, a rock star, and an astronomer—or just waiting patiently for the extraterrestrials to teleport me to limitless galaxies.

But before heading off into outer space, I had to get through university. As any self-respecting young hippie would do, I switched my focus from math and science to theater. The moment I finalized my university schedule, I signed up for my first dance classes. My eccentric beatnik jazz teacher was beyond marvelous, but I had to cap my extra-curricular classes at three per week, to keep up with my theater studies.

I loved the theater and learned invaluable, practical knowledge and powerful life lessons.

Between classes, I lived in the green room, where a regular line-up of classmates waited for their massages on the floor in front of the funky old sofa. Massage was just a natural part of being a child of the 1970s.

Near the end of my first year at university, a friend invited me to a belly dance class. I had no idea what that was, but off we went. I was addicted after the first class, but my future as a belly dancer was cemented when the head of the Theater Department drafted me into the role of Fatima in his production of Rogers and Hammerstein's *Boys from Syracuse*!

Three years later, with my degree and my dance career already established, the big wide world opened its arms to me. The most amazing thing was that I was actually getting paid to do what I loved more than anything else in the world. I decided that I was independently wealthy and that life had no limits to what and where I could create. I spent the next twenty-five years searching, learning, exploring, growing, and delving into a dizzying array of cultures and strange new worlds that had no boundaries thanks to the universality of dance and music.

Eventually, subtle changes in the economy led me to decide to tackle a new career. I applied to the Massage Therapy College in Vancouver. I could not have made a wiser choice for a second career. The next three years were filled with anatomy, physiology, kinesiology, neurology, and pathology, plus a multitude of assessment and massage therapy skills. It was incredibly satisfying to be able to bring people freedom from pain and a return to full, healthy movement.

After so many years living and dancing within my own body, unveiling the mysteries of how all that happened was beyond magical. It revolutionized how I dance and gave me powerful new skills with which to teach. My training in remedial exercise inspired me to completely reinvent my dance class formula. Meanwhile, my life of movement helped me create easy-to-do yet powerfully effective exercises for my clients. I also discovered ways to prevent strain on my body by altering my therapy techniques. Finally, it made sense to me that I was born to a doctor father and a nurse mother—who was also a closet dancer, singer, and pianist!

Now I juggle my two careers. I travel the world to teach dance workshops and intensive professional and instructor training programs, all based on my Body Logic Technique. It might have been tricky to get much more decorative than this! It keeps me young, healthy, joyful, and feeling better than when I was twenty-five!

Then I settle back into my tiny and tranquil village of Lunenburg on the Atlantic Coast of Canada to care for my patients with my own unique approach to massage and manual and movement therapy.

My current project is to put all my trainings into online memberships so that I can help people all over the world enjoy healthy, happy, and pain-free lives! I will also create the first Virtual Belly Dance Festival in the world, and bring my Body Logic for Belly Dancers and Teacher Training Courses to dancers everywhere through online teaching.

ABOUT THE AUTHOR

Jocelyn Chouinard, RMT BA is a Registered Massage Therapist, Instructor; Internationally Renowned Dance Artist, Instructor and Choreographer; Published Writer

My passion is to share the skills and knowledge that she has learned over a lifetime, to help people enjoy a happier, more creative, productive and pain-free life.

As a Therapist, she does this with her hands. She also teach a Series of "S.O.S. Solutions for the Workplace" with Easy to Understand Anatomy for Everyone and Simple Step by Step Systems of Effective Exercises While you Work! As a Teacher of Therapists, she teaches S.O.S. for Therapists to decrease impact on their bodies, as well as CEU Courses in Advanced Massage and Manual Therapy Techniques.

As a dance teacher she teaches beginners to professionals based on my 'Body Logic for Belly Dance Technique'. She also teaches dance teachers a comprehensive 3 year Instructor Training Program. Find out more at: www.kinetherapy.com/

Connect with Jocelyn at:

www.facebook.com/pages/Kinetherapy-Jocelyn-Chouinard-RMT/484027501607314

JUST FREAKIN' DO IT!

By Mike Bayer

H ave you ever seen life slip away in front of you? Have you experienced the strange feeling that comes as you watch what can only be described as the aura fade from another human being? It is a very powerful experience!

For many this happens as they sit at a loved one's bedside, but my experience occurs on a regular basis. Sometimes on the side of a highway. Sometimes on the front lawn of a burning house. Sometimes in the parking lot of a nightclub. No matter what the circumstances, I ask myself the same questions as I ride back to the station in the fire truck after a fatal incident.

Did that person live their life to its fullest? Did that son, father, sister, grandmother have any regrets, anything they wish they had done? What did they put off until retirement? What did they save their entire life to do or experience that will never happen? Did they spend time with their loved ones? Did they travel and see the wonders of the world?

I am not a morbid person; in fact, I am the complete opposite. I freakin' love life! I don't live in fear every time I walk out the door, and I try to take every opportunity, every possibility to experience, every chance to be involved. Why? Because life is too short. We spend too much time worrying about having a career and building a great retirement fund to experience the world, our relationships, and our family in our twilight years. Life throws us curve balls at every turn, and I don't want to wait until retirement to hit the home run because the possibility of a strike out is always there. We get stuck on the treadmill of life, where we just keep working and mostly do not get anywhere. We are just following the same program as everyone else. It works for the majority of people, so why not you, right?

After a few years as a firefighter witnessing the tragic loss of life, I realized that I never want to be limited by commitments. I want to do what I want when I want to and live a life of fulfillment. In the real world, however, everyone has commitments and limitations that hold them back. What held me back, which is the same for millions of people and probably you too, is a simple but soul-destroying phrase: I can't afford it!

I am not going to tell you how to be a millionaire, even though I believe it is within everyone's reach. Instead, I want to tell you that you don't need to be wealthy to live a rich life, a life that is fulfilling and makes you feel whole, proud, and inspired. A life filled with passion for what you love to do and allows you to achieve your personal goals. Saying 'I can't afford it!' is just an excuse and a barrier that you have built to prevent you from breaking away and stepping off the treadmill to experience the beautiful world around you. We work jobs that take us away from our families! We also work very hard at jobs that destroy our relationships. For what? Just to make an extra buck and quite often to make money for someone else.

So what is the plan? How do you put yourself on the track to live the life you should be living, the life you deserve to be living? This is a conversation to have around a campfire with an icebox full of your favorite brew, but here are the basics.

1. Stop thinking that money is the be all and end all to determining your happiness. Money will never get you want you really want, which is freedom. The more money you earn, the more responsibilities and commitments you will develop.

2. Take some time to sit down and think about the root of your passion. What do you wish you could do above all else? What will give you the most fulfillment? Why would you do anything that you don't enjoy? If you have already found your passion, congratulations! If not, every hour you spend doing something you are not passionate about is another hour of your life wasted!

3. What are your priorities to achieve that goal? Are your relationships a strength or a weakness to achieving that goal? This can be the biggest barrier to changing your path. Your decisions may have an impact on not only you but also your partner, family, and friends. How can your change positively impact your relationships? Do you need to change your relationships to achieve your dream? It is your life to live!

4. Do not go blind onto a new path without first doing some planning and preparation! Sometimes a change in life path will cause changes in your financial situation. Ensure you are prepared for this and other changes before making life-altering decisions that could leave you in a bad position. You do not always have to suffer to come out on the other side and achieve success.

5. Write down the steps you need to take to make these changes in your life and the time frame for each step. Be mindful that you choose realistic time goals while still challenging yourself to make the changes you need quickly.

JFDI—Just freakin' do it!

ABOUT THE AUTHOR

Mike is a firefighter in the Greater Toronto Area in Ontario, Canada. After achieving his dream to become a firefighter, he realized this goal only managed to apply the golden handcuffs (a job whose benefits are too good to leave). With a passion for sailing and having just started a new family (two girls under age two in July 2014), Mike and his wife Andrea plan to leave their jobs and take their family sailing around the world. They will follow their passion for family, travel, and freedom. To achieve their new path, they are taking steps to prepare themselves financially with a variety of entrepreneurial endeavors. They are also preparing themselves and the family with the knowledge and skills to not just survive but thrive at sea and in foreign lands. You can follow their stories of self-discovery and their path to freedom in life through their many channels:

www.sailingblogger.com
www.facebook.com/sailingblogger
www.youtube.com/sailingblogger
twitter.com/sailingblogger

THE WE CAN'T SELL ANYTHING MYTH

By Judit Mueller-Kiss

I remember summers in Hungary, where I grew up. My father was a wonderful gardener, tending diligently to its care on days off from his job. He used organic techniques long before organic was fashionable. I have vivid memories of those gardens. The luscious big cherries, sweet as honey, succulent, juicy, and crunchy. One of the last photos of my father was of him climbing the big cherry tree to pick those amazing fruits. Oh, how I loved them!

Some years we had so many we would get bellyaches trying to eat them all. The apples were heavy on the trees, and deep violet grapes on vines drooped to the ground. We always had an abundance of fresh fruits and vegetables, far more than our family of four would ever eat or conserve.

My father hated to allow any fruit to rot on the ground. He was strictly against wasting anything of value, especially food. He begged our neighbors to share in our bounty but few came. Early each weekend, we would help him load his bicycle with the excess produce, and he would head off to the market.

That evening, after the markets closed, he returned with most of his stock still in tow, disappointment in his face. My mother would offer consolation but remind him that "we cannot sell anything." He would nod, agreeing with her. The following week, however, with low expectations and sadness in his heart for all that would likely spoil, he pedaled off again.

"We can't sell anything" was one of our family myths, fed regularly during the summer and autumn months, when produce was abundant in our garden. As a child, these failed trips to the market meant no extra treats for my brother and me. It deeply impressed something on me. My father likened it to a witch sitting on his shoulders, bringing him bad luck in selling. The maxim "We cannot sell anything" rang throughout my life. And there seemed to be no escaping the witch.

When it came time for me to pick a career, I steered away from positions that had anything to do with sales. I studied economics, began my career in banking, and soon moved to journalism. I even ventured into accounting to finance my MBA. It may have been mind-numbingly boring, but at least there was no danger of selling—or, shall we say, not selling—anything.

I earned my MBA in Pittsburgh, Pennsylvania, and returned to Hungary. Many companies were vying for me, including a prestigious ad agency. But the idea that "we can't sell anything" rose again, telling me this might be a tad too close to selling. I chose Coca-Cola Amatil and got a high-powered position as Human Resources Director for Hungary. I loved building up a brand-new company culture and human resources system from scratch!

Then, as part of the system I was creating, I was asked to train as a sales rep for a few months to understand the essence of selling Coke. My reaction? I left the company immediately. No way would I humiliate myself as a sales rep who cannot even sell a crate of Fanta. I was sad but the job market was booming, and I never had any issues finding the next well-paying job. Everyone thought I was insane leaving that prestigious and lucrative job, but so strong was my conviction that "we can't sell anything."

I returned to marketing, my first love, and landed my best job ever with Heinz as a Division Manager. Making decisions on product development, advertising, and purchasing thousands of tons of vegetables and fruits—I enjoyed every minute of it. There was one disturbing factor, though: my success was measured on profits. Without sales, there are no profits! This time, my smart solution was to become friends with and support the sales managers in making those sales flow in. I gave them the best conditions, offering gifts and bonuses, and listened to their stories of making big deals for hours on end. They were my fearless heroes doing the impossible: selling the products I managed. I made such an impression that they invited me to join them in client meetings. I refused. I was afraid the witch on my shoulder would spoil the deal, cursing every attempt they made to sell. I came to the conclusion that as long as I stayed in the corporate world, I could protect myself from having to sell.

But life changes. I left work and moved to Germany with my husband to raise our children. I planned to start my own business. When the time came, I had plenty of great ideas and programs, but no one to sell my services. No friendly hero willing to do the dirty work, either. Over and over the words came back to me, "We can't sell anything." My father was no longer with us, but my mother's voice was as sure as it had ever been.

I was generously giving my ideas and teaching clients, but no money was coming in. I felt more and more pressure to sell; I didn't have the luxury of giving up. If I wanted to see cash flow, I had to break through my lifelong belief of not being able to sell anything.

My first sale fell into my lap while I was busy avoiding selling. I had offered a free session to a man named Robert. After the session he was overjoyed with what he learned. "You have done more for me than anyone else I've talked to," he told me. He wanted to pay me. Robert was on disability, so I didn't push it or ask for any more business from him. I simply thanked him and ended the session. Off on vacation, I forgot about his offer and was shocked upon my return to find money in my account. I had sold something without even trying!

Determined to get it right, I took classes, read books, and received coaching. I learned that if I didn't get my own issues straight, I was never going to be able to sell. The key to my change was being able to face the strongly held conviction that "we can't sell anything." I had to leave this belief in the past, change my thinking, and face my inner issues.

If I didn't like being sold to, how could I expect anyone else to? I discovered that it's not about trying to force someone into a sale. My breakthrough moment came when I realized that selling is serving. It means offering to share what you've learned, what you have to give. If I wanted to help my clients have their own breakthroughs, I had to give up my false notions of sales and learn how to sell in a way that worked for me, a way that didn't carry the rotten smell of failure.

I learned that you must believe 100% in what you are selling. If you don't, make your product or service better until you do. Faith in yourself is important, too. If you believe in yourself, you will never devalue what you know or have to offer. In the end, selling means asking, "How can I help you?" This was something I could easily do, since it didn't feel like "selling" as I previously viewed it. It worked for me, and it works for my clients, too.

Persistence is key. My father persisted in packing his produce and taking it to the market every week, even with little hope of success. It wasn't an option for him to stay at home and let the fruit rot, so he persisted.

Likewise, failure wasn't an option for me. I had to ask myself, "Are you willing to do what it takes? Are you willing to let your God-given talents go to waste? Will you let your fear of selling stop you from serving the world?" By sticking with it, I found a way into selling. If I can learn to sell after life-long conditioning that I cannot, anyone can.

Having dealt with internal and external issues, I can now help my clients sell their programs and services. I can show them how to attract ideal prospects, ask for business, and provide the best service they can. As a result, many of my clients have gone on to reach six-figure incomes.

ABOUT THE AUTHOR

Judit Mueller-Kiss helps creative entrepreneurs to profit from their winning ideas. Through playful creativity and solid business principles, she helps them build a constant client flow, providing dependable income. She teaches her clients to sell with confidence and ease and find great joy and satisfaction in their businesses.

Find out more about Judit at creativitysage.com.

Connect with Judit at:

twitter.com/CreativitySage

de.linkedin.com/in/juditmuellerkiss/en

http://www.facebook.com/juditmuellerkiss

IF YOU TRULY WANT SOMETHING, NOTHING CAN STOP YOU

by Kathy Pop

I have met some absolutely amazing people in my life, but the two that have influenced me most overcame huge physical challenges and are living proof that we all can do anything we want to!

These two influential women were born without limbs. One is a lawyer and lives independently, with a home health aid visiting for just one hour each day. She was featured on the Disability Network TV in the early 1990s. The documentary showed her dressing herself and putting on makeup. With two arms, I can't even put eyeliner on, but she can. This woman is amazing.

The other woman is a single mom and earns a living playing the keyboard on Atlantic City's boardwalk. She was determined to earning a living doing anything she could. Being on public assistance was out of the question for her.

When I learned of these women, I was a Certified Mental Health Specialist and worked with folks with multiple handicaps. I showed the programs to my clients to inspire them to keep going, to achieve their goals and not give up. I liked helping people achieve greater independence and find jobs they enjoyed and excelled at.

I grew up in an entrepreneurial family, but that was not their plan for me. They hoped that I would have a job as a doctor or a veterinarian, with a nice benefits package and retirement plan. I'm sure they often wonder where they went wrong. I've always been an independent thinker, which made me the black sheep of the family. I have played the role of caretaker most of my life. I was the one in the family who would quit her job to care for a relative when needed, so I worked for myself most of my life.

I started working for myself forty years ago this year. I was sixteen years old and joined a 4-H dog club. Neighbors saw me training my dog and asked me to train theirs. I have been training dogs most of my life.

My father raised beagles as hunting dogs, and when I was old enough to run, my father asked me to drag a scent dummy around the yard so our beagles could track it. I thought I was just playing hide and seek with them.

I have started several businesses over the years, but just as they were beginning to do well, something would happen forcing me to either quit or cut back. Most of the time it was because the health of one of my relatives took a nosedive, and they needed help.

I closed a business in the mid 1980s after I was raped. I knew the man. He had serious emotional problems. He continued to harass and stalk me, making it impossible to conduct business. He was delusional, thinking we were getting married. He drove my clients and staff away. Then I found out I was pregnant. I had no health insurance and could not obtain insurance coverage because it was considered a pre-existing condition. The only real choice I had was to close the business.

I took advantage of the next four years to get my act together. The stories of the two women I mentioned earlier helped me regain my confidence and plan for the future. If women with no arms or legs could provide for themselves and find success, then what was I capable of achieving?

I returned to college and became a Certified Mental Health Specialist. I became a mentor, instructor, and advocate for people with disabilities. I waited to start another business, so my son would have health insurance. I was also unsure if my son's father would show up again, since it took almost two years to get him out of our lives.

In 1996, my father was losing his battle with lymphoma and needed help. He was still running two businesses: a small bar and apartments in the same building. I quit my job to help him physically and with the businesses. I only got a crash course in the day-to-day operations and liquor laws for the bar business. He passed away less than three months after I started helping him.

I had my work cut out for me. The building was built in the late 1800s and needed a lot of work. Some documents were still in my grandfather's name. I found out he was Customer #3 for the electric company.

The bar business was a mess. My father's employees had taken full advantage of his growing absence and inability to manage it properly. I finally turned it around and tripled the revenue. Then I sold the liquor license and building in 2003. The neighborhood had declined and there were outstanding issues surrounding my father's estate, which still had not been settled.

I began doing consulting work with other bar and restaurant owners and managers. I realized that the Internet was just beginning and was going to be a huge place for businesses, so I found a group that used web conferencing to teach Internet marketing and online business. I learned whatever I could and then began teaching it to others. I really enjoy teaching and coaching, so that is my current focus.

I now use those experiences and creative problem solving to help others make their life's dreams a reality. I love learning new things. I also love sharing what I have learned with others.

I love the technology we have now! It allows almost anyone anywhere to start a business. It's an awesome feeling to walk someone through a task they thought was too complicated. I love to see their eyes light up and hear the joy in their voices when they get it.

I have had plenty of losses and devastating events in my life, including being stalked and raped. I was also homeless once. These events made me a stronger and more compassionate person. My struggles have taught me to help others overcome their own struggles and live the life they always dreamed they could have.

The two women taught me that we all have challenges in life. Some are visible and others are not, but if you truly want something, nothing can stop you. Whenever I felt like throwing in the towel, I think back on the obstacles these women have had to overcome. Even when I made a stupid mistake or it just seems too hard, I realize my problems are not as challenging as theirs. If they can do it, then any one of us can, too.

We are all destined for greatness! It may be a rough road, filled with ups and downs, but the final destination makes it all worth it. What kind of awesomeness will your journey bring?

ABOUT THE AUTHOR

Kathy Pop uses her forty years experience as an Entrepreneur to help people create amazing online businesses as a Coach and Trainer. She considers her clients to be a part of her extended family. Helping them be successful is what families do for each other, isn't it?

She loves finding creative solutions to ordinary problems and bringing out what makes you unique and special so that you stand out from everyone else.

Find out more about Kathy at kathypop.com

Connect with Kathy at:

facebook.com/kathypop

twitter.com/kathypop

linkedin.com/in/kathypop

plus.google.com/+KathyPop

STARTING OTHER'S STORIES

By Leeza Robertson

---

t was a cold and overcast November day in the Las Vegas Valley, and I found myself sitting on the floor surrounded by scraps of paper. Just me and a bunch of half-scribbled pieces of paper, hardly a scene of impending success. I was about to shut the door on a business I had spent the last five years building. I would shift my attention to a side business that I wanted to grow and be my sole focus.

As I sat there, I wondered if I could really do this, or if I was setting myself up for self-sabotage. As an entrepreneur, it can be hard to tell the difference between a calculated risk and self-sabotage. Like all risks, only time would tell if what I was about to do would pay off in the long run.

I looked around at this nonsensical collection of papers and took a deep breath and closed my eyes. Instantly I was transported to the Australian Bush of my childhood. I was on my bike, riding as fast as I could. No destination, no expectations, just freedom and an endless horizon. It would be an understatement to say it was flat as a pancake where I grew up. The only thing I had to worry about when I was riding my bike was the odd brown snake sunning itself in the middle of the road.

Snakes—I am terrified of them and the life-changing energy they carry. Yet there I was, in the year of the snake, remembering the snakes of my youth as I contemplated the need to shed my old ways and start all over again. How ironic, I thought.

I kept my eyes closed and took another deep breath as I conjured that vision of freedom again—just me, my bike, and vast open space. I needed to get into a deeper place with this energy of limitless potential, to truly befriend the notion of no expectations. I was starting anew—well sort of—and it was risky and exciting all at the same time.

Taking another deep breath, I opened my eyes and took another look at the scattered pieces of paper around me. It was time to pull on my big girl pants and get serious. I had an amazing business coach, a fantastic publishing contract, and the most supportive partner in the world. What could possibly go wrong?

Boy, that was the worst question to ask. I suddenly saw every failed attempt and heard every person who had ever told me I couldn't, shouldn't, and didn't deserve it all. They rushed into the room with a suffocating energy.

"Shake it off," I told myself. "You are not that person anymore. You can do this. You have a massive support team, and people believe in you."

I was actually starting to think that might be the problem. My whole over-achieving life had been set up to prove other people wrong. What would I do now that everyone was on my side?

What a dilemma. It wasn't one I ever thought I would have to deal with, but there I was, slipping out of my old self and standing raw in a new skin I didn't know how to wear.

Taking yet another deep breath, I looked around the room in a panic and hoped like hell that the answer I was looking for was somehow encoded on this mishmash of papers I found surrounding me.

I guess it was my lucky day. There on the floor in that ocean of paper and ink were the makings of a list of all the different forms of writing, the many ways content could be published and delivered to the marketplace, and a huge list of all the moving parts many new authors know nothing about. This was it, this was the new journey. The best part was I could do it without getting out of my pajamas or leaving the house. These things are important to extreme introverts like me.

Over the previous several years, I had been working very closely with new authors as a side business. I began to see that there was so much information that authors really needed access to, that there were huge gaps in many writers' knowledge of publishing. I also noticed that they needed it from experts in each area of publishing. Though I did my best to keep my private clients and students up-to-date with the publishing options available to authors, I soon realized it was more than I could possibly cram into the programs and services I was offering.

I was, however, only one woman, and I needed a tribe. The first step to building my own tribe was to figure out whom I wanted to join. I didn't know it at the time, but there is no finite answer to that question. As your tribe begins to grow and form, so too do the needs and dynamics of the people you pull into it. You don't lose or change your vision for your tribe, but you shift the parameters of who you will allow to join it.

Let me give you an example of how my tribe has shifted and evolved since its inception. I primarily work with women; it is how I have shaped this business, and I am in no hurry to change that. I do also have male clients, but they are few and far between. When I was thinking about putting together my dream tribe of experts, I wanted to keep this feminine focus flowing. I initially only contacted female experts to showcase to my market.

But I hit a problem. In some areas men were doing a better job than women. Knowing I wanted to stay aligned to my vision of delivering the best possible content to educate my market, I had to be flexible with the parameters of my tribe, so I started adding more men.

I am still adding to my tribe as you read this. It is an ongoing process, and it has bought amazing opportunities. I have made many new friends and created some awesome joint ventures. Not to mention it has opened doors to people, places, and possibilities I would never have had access to if I did not take this journey. For an extreme introvert, this tribe thing has done wonders for my credibility and my visibility.

The best part about building your own tribe is to let go of the need to know it all and to be all things to all people. You soon learn that each member has an area of exceptional knowledge. It is each person's area of expertise that makes them significant. Building my tribe has allowed me to showcase that significance in both my tribe and my clients.

How did I find my tribe members? The short answer is stalking. I highly recommend it, as it has paid off for me. I don't mean creepy stalking; that will land you in jail (and rightly so). What I mean is to know everything you can about the people you approach. Follow them on social media, read (and comment) on their blogs, and add yourself to their mailing list. Try to be introduced to them via common contacts. The more you know about someone, the more inclined they are to work with you. Stroking your potential tribe member's ego doesn't hurt either. Make it all about them, and show them you know exactly how you can serve their needs first.

On that cold winter day back in the year of the snake, I wasn't just looking to start the next chapter of my story. I was looking at how I could start the next chapter of other people's stories. I was diving deep into the possibility of creating a movement, one that would tap into the significance of story-telling with as many voices as possible.

Closing my eyes yet again, I returned to the vision of my youth and felt the wind caress my face. I could not have known that 25 years later I would be calling on that part of my story to share with others. Here it is, and that is how I created my business around the belief that your story matters.

Tell it and share it, but most of all, write it.

ABOUT THE AUTHOR

 Leeza Robertson is a bestselling author, expert book coach, speaker and intuitive. Over the past several years she's been blessed to take some amazing women and the occasional man on a journey that changed their lives forever. They went from thinking that being a published author was out of their reach to being up on Amazon in twelve weeks. They went from a place of, 'I can't ' to a place of "Let's do it again!" Some even went from unknown to bestseller in under seven days. Leeze enjoys helping others have this level of success.

Learn more about Leeza and how you can work with her at: leezarobertson.com

Connect with Leeza at:

facebook.com/CreatingBestsellingAuthors

twitter.com/Leeza_Robertson

LEARNING TO LIVE FROM THE HEART

By Kay Rice

M y trip to Peru took on a life of its own. It started before I left the United States; situations, circumstances, and opportunities indicated that a force was at work directing my life. Having learned it is best not to argue with the Universe, I stood back and watched as my life unfolded. When my computer crashed the week before I left, I was grateful. I had time to get if fixed before I left and it was running better than ever. Then it crashed again the day after I arrived in the Sacred Valley of Peru. Apparently the Universe had decided I needed to focus on my journey rather than the Internet.

I received an invitation to go to Machu Picchu before I left the U.S. I didn't have to plan a thing. The guide, the hotel, and all the arrangements had been made. All I had to do was say yes. Imagine, a trip to Machu Picchu planned without having to even think about it. I knew I'd get there only eight days after arriving in Peru.

Lake Titicaca was also on my bucket list. It is located in the southernmost part of Peru and northern Bolivia. I knew very little

Spanish, so it would be difficult for me to go there alone. One day I was told three times that I should go to Lake Titicaca, specifically to the Isla del Sol, or Island of the Sun, on the Bolivian side. At the end of the day, a woman named Donna approached me and said she would be taking a group to Lake Titicaca in a few weeks. After her group left, she would travel into Bolivia and go to the Island of the Sun. She said she had received a very strong message to invite me to come with her. And so it was!

I joined her group on the last few days of their tour and traveled to Puno with them. From there, Donna and I crossed the border into Bolivia. We had been given the name of a man named Rojer, an Aymara Shaman who lived on the remote side of the Island of the Sun. We were to take a ferry from the peninsula of Copacabana to Cha'lla to meet Rojer, who spoke no English. We depended on Donna's Spanish for directions. Earlier in the day Donna had commented that she wanted to improve her Spanish, so instead of merely thinking she understood what people were saying, she wanted to be sure she really understood. As a result of some miscommunication, however, we missed the commercial ferry to the island and had to charter our own boat to a destination called Cha'lla. We did not know there was a "Cha'lla 1" and a "Cha'lla 2."

When we arrived, our boatman quickly unloaded our luggage and sped away. Rojer was nowhere in sight. There are no motorized vehicles on the Island of the Sun, and the terrain is steep and rocky. We had no way to contact Rojer, no way off the island, and it appeared we had been dropped off in the middle of nowhere.

In the distance some children were tending animals. A boy approached us. Donna explained we were looking for Rojer. He replied, "Sí, sí, conozco a Rojer,"—Yes, I know Rojer—pointing in the direction of the steep rocky terrain in the distance. Rojer lived on the other side of that mountain, at Cha'lla 2; we had been dropped off at Cha'lla 1.

Clearly, we had a problem. Not only was it a significant distance and a steep climb, but we also had to carry our luggage. It seemed unlikely we could make it over the mountain hauling our belongings, so Donna asked the young man if he had friends who we could pay to carry our luggage. He said no and quickly left. Donna and I took off in the direction he had indicated, across the field. Another boy ran to us and said the path to get over the mountain was in a different direction. Donna asked him if he would run over the mountain and tell Rojer we had arrived so he could help us with our bags. The boy answered, "No, I must watch my animals."

We had two weeks of luggage we were hauling on foot. We were at a very high altitude, which made it much more physically challenging. We had no food, no water, and no shelter. As soon as the sun set, the temperature would plummet. We were in a potentially dangerous situation if we didn't get over the mountain and find Rojer before dark. I didn't know whether to be amused or annoyed that Donna kept stopping to ask people to help us. It was obvious to me that we were responsible for ourselves and our luggage. We didn't have much time before the sun would set. Donna grumbled along the way, asking herself why she had brought all of these belongings and considered leaving them on the path. We were both exhausted when we reached the courtyard at the top of the mountain. As we headed down the other side of the rocky path, we found Rojer on the path waiting for us.

He led us to the hostel on the beach where we would stay for the next several days. Victoria and Francisco, our hosts, served us one of the most delicious meals I had yet eaten in South America. Delicious fish, roasted vegetables, potatoes, and tea! As we finished our meal I could hear the waves lapping on the shore.

After our dinner, Rojer escorted us to our room, where he performed an opening ceremony for our time together. We breathed our intentions into coca leaves and placed them around our room to create sacred space. Rojer cleared our energy fields using a feather from a great condor. We heard the feather move through the air as if the great bird were flying in the room. When he finished, he stood in front of me for a moment and exclaimed, "You are a butterfly!" Then he looked at Donna and asked, "Don't you see that she is a butterfly?" Then, looking more serious, he told me, "There are many great teachers around you. They have been there for a long time. Osho, Gandhi, Carl Jung, James Campbell, and others. But you are blocked."

As Rojer left, he told us he would be back for us in a few hours. We should be prepared to leave well before daylight in the morning. We would hike further up the rocky terrain and arrive at our next destination well before sunrise. There we would perform a ceremony. It would be very cold, but he promised to build "un fuego"—a fire—for us when we arrived.

He called in all the elements and all the Apus (mountain guardians) and prayed for all the countries and peoples of the earth. He honored our ancestors, mother earth, and father sky. He beat his drum, chanted, and conducted ceremony for more than an hour as the sun rose. Finally, we stood with our eyes closed on the rocky cliff overlooking Lake Titicaca in the direction of the newly risen sun. Afterward Rojer asked each of us what we had seen. I described an image that I did not know until later is a symbol of the eye of the condor. He looked pleased.

After our ceremony Rojer explained the four spiritual gateways on the Isla del Sol. We passed the first gateway by boat. We passed the second gateway when we were dropped off at the wrong Cha'lla and had to climb the mountain. Today we were at the location of the third gateway, where we accepted the spiritual path. He warned, "Not everyone who accepts the spiritual path will fly! So where are your feathers? Where are your feathers?" Showing us his feathers, he explained that our first feathers would come to us; we would either find them in nature or we would be gifted them; they could not be purchased.

As we stood to leave, Rojer looked at me and said, "Your block is in your head. You do not need to read any more books. I know Osho, Carl Jung, and Gandhi; I know many great teachers. I have never read their books. Stop using your head so much; instead you must learn to use your heart to think."

I found my feathers. The first were hummingbird feathers. Now I have many feathers and have discovered the magic and flow when you learn to live from the heart rather than the head.

ABOUT THE AUTHOR

My journey is a story about learning to live from the heart. If you would like to learn what it is to truly use the "power of intention" to dream the life you want into existence, then my story may interest you. My journey has taken me from health & fitness, through learning the key success principles, to learning Mind-Body-Spirit principles and techniques from Deepak Chopra and other teachers, to traveling to South America to live while learning the Spiritual and Healing traditions of the Andes.

Kay is a Speaker, Author and Certified Wellness & Lifestyle Coach. She has a Masters Degree in Exercise Physiology, is a Certified Wellness and Lifestyle Coach, Chopra Center Certified Instructor, Reiki Master

www.kayrice.com

www.EverythingIsAnInsideJob.com

www.YourHolidayFeast.com

Connect with Kay at:

facebook.com/kayhrice

twitter.com/kay_rice

www.linkedin.com/in/kayrice

plus.google.com/u/0/+KayRice/posts/p/pub

THE RISE FROM ADVERSITY

By Keitha Maciel

"**Y**ou've got to be joking. Where's Ashton Kutcher? I know I'm being 'Punk'd'!" Then a slow chuckle turned into a continuous laugh because I could not believe what had just happened. I had to laugh to keep from crying.

I can remember that day vividly—the day my husband told me he was laid off from his job. People get laid off all the time. But what made that situation different was that I had lost my job on Friday, just three days before. My heart started pounding faster, and I began to breathe heavy. I thought to myself, What are we going to do? We had a mortgage, two car payments, and other credit card debt. I saw everything that we had worked for snatched from us.

I looked for a job daily, to no avail. My heart was heavy with anxiety for the fear of losing everything. I lived numb during that time. I continued with normal activities, but I wasn't really present or feeling what was going on. I did not realize it at the time, but I was depressed.

My husband and I continued to look for jobs, but a couple months later salt was poured into the wound. My brother was sick and needed to vacate his apartment. My mother was already living with us, and she said, "We've got to go down and get him." I said, "But Mom, I don't know how <u>we</u> are going to make it, let alone house and feed another person." She said, "You have to pray and rely on God." So we brought my brother to live with us. It turned out he had Aspiration Pneumonia and had to be hospitalized. Fortunately, he eventually recovered.

But the bad news didn't stop there. A few months after my brother moved in, while I was still unemployed, my dog, Cookie, stopped eating. I felt a tumor in her belly. I was so sad because Cookie was only three years old, rescued from an animal shelter, and I wasn't ready for her to die. My mother paid for her to see the vet, and he confirmed that she had a tumor. Fortunately, she eventually recovered, too.

The Light at the End of the Tunnel

We had four adults and two dogs living in a house, and no one was working. I realized I needed to start a business. I did not want to rely on a corporate job that I could lose again. I told myself, "I need a Plan B." I began helping small business owners with their marketing. Friends and family were already coming to me for business and marketing advice. It seemed like a natural transition to start a consulting business.

The challenge was that I still had no money to advertise and market myself. We were living off unemployment benefits, which did not cover all the bills. I didn't feel I could take the money for household expenses to market my business. I continued looking for a regular job. I told myself, "If I find a job, that money will help fund my business."

In the interim, I decided to go back to school. I had the time, and I used financial aid to pay for my education. I found a specialized program for Internet marketing. I knew that the Internet would be the way of the future, and it provided me with skills and knowledge in an area where I was lacking. I completed the program with a Master's degree in Internet Marketing.

This new knowledge and skill would help me in my business. I could offer these services to help other entrepreneurs, solopreneurs (for example, authors, consultants, and lawyers), and small business owners market themselves online. The Internet was not going away. Businesses that didn't leverage the Internet as a revenue stream were leaving money on the table and missing out on a tool that could be used to drive income.

I set out on a journey to build a business helping others grow their businesses. I learned three valuable insights about business along the way.

The first is that you have to thoroughly understand your customer/client or target audience. Why is understanding your potential buyers so important? The obvious answer is that they are the bread and butter of any business. Without people to buy your product or service, you have no business. Therefore, it is to your advantage to know your prospective customer well. You will be able to develop relevant and attention-grabbing messaging, sales, and marketing materials.

Research studies show that consumers buy on emotion. How do you engage your customers' emotions? The key is in the messaging. The words you use in your ads, your brochures, your web site, and other marketing and sale pieces can either engage or repel a consumer. Effective messaging can help you influence buying behavior and move people to action.

Messaging can be a powerful differentiator. There are very few differences between products and services today. What will encourage you to choose one over the other? One factor is the brand. The second factor is packaging. Third, what you say about your product or service.

Along my journey, I discovered the importance of messaging and the power of words, so I set out to master messaging. I enrolled in several copywriting courses from expert copywriters. I also attended Robert Cialdini's Principles of Persuasion workshop. I wanted to learn how to put influence to work.

The second key business insight I learned along my journey was to differentiate yourself by building a strong brand. Your brand is how people perceive you and your business in the market; it will help you stand out from the competition. Your brand involves all aspects of your business. It is not just your logo and color scheme.

Solopreneurs need a brand, too. Personal branding has two main benefits: it establishes your reputation and credibility and it distinguishes you from your peers and competitors. Ultimately, your goal with a personal brand is to demonstrate to potential buyers and prospective clients why they should choose you. I help entrepreneurs and solopreneurs build their brand by monetizing their expertise. I help them create information, products, and digital packages to sell online.

This leads me to the third business insight: any person in business today must have an online presence. In addition to a web site, a marketing system and a process to promote your product/service online is essential. There are millions of web sites on the Internet; if no one can find your business online within the first few pages of a search engine like Google, Yahoo, or Bing, you're missing opportunities to make money.

There is a science to online marketing. Once you know what to do, you can replicate your actions to create predictable results.

"At the end of the day…"

If you read the biographies of very successful business owners, you will see that most of them had to overcome some obstacle or adversity to achieve their goals. But each had a burning desire to succeed that helped them persevere through the trials and tribulation.

Adversity and obstacles will be placed before you. It's not the adversity or obstacle that will prevent you from achieving your goal, it's how you react to it. As you can see, I did not let the adversity paralyze me. Instead, I started a company called Income Boosters.

Thanks to God, through faith and prayer, I was able to rise from adversity.

ABOUT THE AUTHOR

Keitha Maciel is a marketing and branding professional who helps businesses promote their brand, attract new customers and generate revenue. For over twelve years, she has launched marketing campaigns and developed product messaging for solopreneurs, small businesses and Fortune 500 companies to help them generate revenue and distinguish themselves from the competition. Keitha is the author of the forthcoming book, "A.C.E. Marketing- 3 Essential Strategies for Sustainable Business Growth." She has a master's degree in Internet marketing from Full Sail University and keeps current with the latest trends and techniques.

Find out more about Keitha at www.incomeboosters.com

Connect with Keitha at:

facebook.com/incomeboosters

twitter.com/KeithaMaciel

THE FARMER'S SPIRIT

By Laura Wagner

I t was a great day! But it was also an uncertain and scary day. It was April 16, 1997. Our cows walked out of the barn for the last time; we were no longer dairy farmers. We had just made a life-changing decision. Would it prove to be the right choice?

My husband Joe and I managed our dairy farm and milked cows for twenty years. For the latter half of those years, we struggled with stray voltage, an insidious phenomenon that has destroyed whole herds and their owners. Our case wasn't quite that bad; it didn't kill our cattle or cause health issues for us. It did, however, cause health problems in our cows, which resulted in lower milk production. Because our income was based on pounds of milk produced, it hurt our bottom-line when any cow did not produce to standards.

Several times we consulted with the electric company. We were first told we didn't have a problem. We knew better but didn't know how to prove it. We were later told we indeed had stray voltage but they didn't know how to correct it. Over the years, we also worked with several nutritionists. When we followed their suggestions, the cows suffered from diarrhea or swollen knees, were in pain, and produced less milk.

Our herd size and income dropped each year. Normally older cows are replaced by heifers when they give birth to their first calf, but many of our cows were leaving the barn years earlier than they should due to poor health and low milk production. We couldn't raise replacement heifers fast enough.

After years of guessing, we installed a water meter in the barn to determine how much water the cows were drinking each day. We weren't completely shocked to learn they were drinking approximately one-third to one-half the gallons a herd that size should be drinking. We concluded some cows were getting a shock every time they took a drink from the metal drinking cup. They learned to drink only the minimum to stay alive, not enough for good health or milk production. It was devastating to realize we were subjecting our animals to this every day.

We were faced with a choice. We could re-wire the entire barn, which would substantially add to our large farm debt, or we could sell our cows. My husband and I were both tired of the day-to-day grind and stress of milking cows. We had been milking morning and evening, seven days a week, with no vacation for twenty years. It was nearly impossible to take time off because cows know when someone different is milking. That alone can drop production. We simply couldn't afford a vacation.

What's more, in 1997, our children were ages sixteen, fourteen, twelve and eight, and they were involved in many school activities. Milking often kept us from attending those events.

At the same time, Joe was presented the opportunity to start his own construction business. It wasn't an easy choice, but we hoped we knew what was best for our family. Joe continued farming our 200 acres, selling the crops rather than storing them for feed, and worked construction when not planting and harvesting. I was halfway through a four-year term as Clerk/Treasurer for our local municipality. Along with helping on the farm and raising four kids, the Clerk job kept me busy. I saw myself as Clerk/Treasurer for many years to come.

That changed on October 4, 1998. I remember the day well because it happened to be my 40th birthday! The new Town Chairman informed me I would be replaced as Clerk/Treasurer when my term expired the following April. It was devastating news because I had worked hard, computerized all the town records, learned a lot about municipal government, and thoroughly loved the job!

As the saying goes, when one door closes, another one opens. I had to find the other door, but I had no idea where it was or what it looked like. I enrolled in computer classes at Moraine Park Technical College (MPTC). I didn't know if I'd find the right door there, but I had discovered my love for computers when working as Clerk/Treasurer and I wanted to learn more. Sometimes it's the simple choices that turn out to make the biggest differences in our lives.

I didn't attend college after high school because it wasn't what I wanted at that time in my life. I wanted to work, save money, get married, and have a family. A stay-at-home mom raised me and that is what I wanted for my family. With my first classes at MPTC, I had a lot to learn about college.

In the summer of 2000 I enrolled in two classes in MPTC's newly formed Web Developer program. I took HTML and Photoshop so I could make a website for my friend's business. I soon realized there was much more to web development than I could learn in two classes, and I enjoyed web design so much. I was hooked. By December 2002, I had earned a Technical Diploma and Associate's Degree.

In 2003, I enrolled in classes at Lakeland College to earn a Bachelor's degree but after just one semester, I again faced difficult choices. I wondered if I was wasting time and money when I could be working and bringing in a paycheck. I chose to take a break from school while working a temporary job to figure out the answers.

I bounced around the job world during these years, with some good and some very bad experiences. Every job taught me what I wanted and, more importantly, what I didn't want. I didn't want a job in retail. I didn't want a secretarial job. I didn't want a job I'd be bored with after six months. Every job seemed to push me toward my own business.

I went back to Lakeland College, and by December 2005, I was a college graduate with a Bachelor's Degree in Computer Science! It was a lot of work for five years but it speaks to my tenacity and stubbornness. No one said I must. No one said I should. In fact, most family and friends probably thought I was a little crazy pursuing the degree at my age.

After earning my Bachelor's degree, I taught as an adjunct instructor at MPTC, where I had started the Web Developer program years earlier. As fate would have it, I had many women students in their forties and fifties who had lost their jobs. I gave them some hope for the future. If I could do it, they could too! I told them to think about the bigger picture of their futures. Most of them had worked in a factory for 10 or 20 years and couldn't imagine themselves doing anything else. I wanted them to understand they had many years yet to work, so they shouldn't settle for a boring job.

You don't need to earn a college degree. There are so many learning opportunities on the Internet. Find something you love, as I found computers and web development, and seek out ways to learn more. If you have thoughts of owning your own business, there are people to help you. Start with your local technical college, where you will find helpful staff with many ideas and resources. They will direct you to others who can help. Don't wait until you have a solid plan because that day may never come. Just get started, and your path and your plan will become apparent.

I continue to study and learn to keep up with my rapidly changing industry, and I have built a strong Website development business with loyal customers. For twenty years I expected I would be milking cows until retirement. When we sold the cows and I lost my Clerk/Treasurer position, I faced the question, Now what? What would I do with the rest of my life?

Throughout those years, I was taken in many directions, but I kept returning to web development. Sometimes learning what you don't want is just as important as learning what you do want.

I know now the independent work lifestyle is the one for me. Perhaps it's the farmer spirit that became ingrained in my being. When I look back, there was never a definite plan. I just kept looking for the next door to open and pursued it to the end.

ABOUT THE AUTHOR

 Laura Wagner formed her web design business, Webs by Wagner in 2003 after earning an Associate's Degree in Web Development. She then continued her schooling, earning a Bachelor's degree in Computer Science.

Wagner now also offers online marketing services and mobile website development. She continues to perfect her web design skills while building a strong business with loyal customers.

The strong work ethic Laura learned growing up has been enhanced through 30+ years of helping her husband on their family farm and raising four children. She brings that work ethic, along with great sense of responsibility, to each Web project.

Find out more about Laura at websbywagner.com

Connect with Laura at:

facebook.com/websbywagner

facebook.com/lauragwagner

linkedin.com/in/lauragwagner

google.com/+LauraWagner

THE POWER OF NETWORKING

By Natalie Marie Collins

saw it coming for months. The oil and gas project I was working on was winding down and would soon come to an end. Several other projects had recently ended abruptly, and we were given 30 days to wrap them up.

One day my boss walked in and solemnly broke the news to the office that the project was getting shut down. We had about two weeks to wrap it up, and there were no other projects coming down the pipeline. Translation: You have two weeks until you will be out of a job. Better start looking.

I felt a tinge of panic come over me. What would I do for money? How would I be able to afford my house payment, car payment, daycare, and everything else that comes with being a responsible adult and parent?

Or was it excitement I felt? My entrepreneurial life could officially start full-time. Yes, it was nervous excitement. After thirteen years I was finally being released from the corporate office environment. I felt almost giddy knowing I wouldn't have to come into an office everyday, sit in corner, and work on things I didn't enjoy.

My boss pulled me into his office. I had been his assistant for nearly eight years. We worked well together, and I appreciated how he believed in me and supported my growth and learning. It was sad to know that our time working together had come to an end. He said, "You know that if I have work, you have work, but I don't even have any. I'm sorry."

I left the office that day with a smile, knowing he had done everything he could, but it was time for me to go out on my own. To do what, I wasn't sure yet. I knew I had about two months' worth of savings to figure it out. I also knew I wouldn't be going back to the corporate office environment. It was time to get serious.

Over the previous year I had started to learn about online processes, product creation, websites, list management systems, copywriting, and marketing from my then-boyfriend (now husband), Lee. I had met some amazing, fun, and genuine people who were helping me learn even more. I learned about the power of masterminds and knew I was in the right place.

In fact, during my first marketing event, I remember being overjoyed to realize that the people around me thought the same way I did. That this was where they had all been hiding. From then on I was hooked and fascinated with how online marketing worked.

The list management systems and membership sites were easy for me to learn because they are essentially online databases. They were similar to what I had been working with and managing in Corporate America. I caught on really quickly. One of my entrepreneurial friends realized this and asked me to help with her website backend, email list, and membership site. She asked me to become her virtual assistant. The best part was she would happily pay me to do it!

I couldn't say no to earning money for work I enjoyed. I also loved working with someone who inspired me everyday to build a business around what I'm good at and enjoy doing. I told her about what happened with my corporate job. Then something amazing started happening.

She started to hustle work for me. She started telling her other entrepreneurial friends and clients about me. I was amazed at how open and vocal she was about it. In fact, she wasn't the only one. Lee was also helping me look for people to help. I instantly had a small community of people who believed in me and knew what I could do, helping me find my niche. Most importantly, I was able to help them, which generated money to pay the bills.

By chance, through an old friend of Lee's and new friend of mine, I was introduced to Joel Comm, who needed help compiling a book. I am a writer at heart and was happy to help him with the administrative side of organizing the authors and the book itself. Joel hired me to become his virtual assistant.

Within two months I was able to acquire a few more clients, and between all of them, I was able to bring in enough income to pay my bills and do things I enjoyed.

During this time I realized the power of association. Had it not been for my relationships with other people, chances are I would not have gotten what I needed in the short amount of time I did.

This brings me to the saying, "It's not what you know, it's who you know." This is true, in a sense, but without my knowledge and background, it would not have mattered who I knew if I couldn't do the work.

Once I had the skills to help effectively, others recommended me because were confident in my ability to do what I said I could. They knew I could do the work. Even friends don't want to put their name on the line for someone they don't trust to do what they say they can. If you really know your stuff and you've been able to prove it to your friends and associates, they will happily tell others about you, and you will gain the recommendations you need to succeed.

Back to the saying, "It's not what you know, it's who you know." To that I say, "It's what you know AND who you know" that catapults you to the next level.

The power of networking has proven itself to me time and time again. Even when I have a full client load, I am willing to discuss with people their needs for a virtual assistant. I believe in leaving the doors open to opportunities that are better than I could have imagined them to be.

ABOUT THE AUTHOR

 Natalie Marie Collins is a Virtual Assistant and doodling creative who is passionate about online product creation and building a solid business backend and membership areas. Her ability to write fun support desk auto responses helped turn cries for help into smiles and giggles. She is also the Co-Founder of the VA Success School, teaching other Virtual Assistants the tools their clients need them to know and how to boost their business and grow their happy client roster.

Discover how Natalie uses her doodles in business at NatalieMarieCollins.com.

Connect with Natalie at:

www.facebook.com/natmariecollinspage/

twitter.com/NatMarieCollins

www.linkedin.com/in/nataliemariecollins/

YOUR OBSTACLES ARE YOUR UNIQUE EDGE

By Marybeth Rosato

P acing back and forth in my foyer, I heard car doors slam outside my home. Seeing the five women walk up my driveway brought on a mild panic attack. It felt like the enemy was approaching in slow motion. Heart racing and unable to think straight, I remember saying aloud to myself, "Why did I ever get mixed up in something like this? Who do I think I am?" All of the 'less than' thoughts I believed about myself growing up came flooding back. These women would soon see through my polished exterior, would find out I wasn't good enough, and confirm all the negative beliefs I carried around most of my life.

It may be laughable to you that this seemingly-small event could cause someone this much duress, but for me it was real. Even as I write this I relive it. What is it, you wonder, that could create so much stress? Believe it or not, it was my first home party.

I was twenty-seven years old, married a little over two years, had just delivered my first child, and left my company and moved to a new state so my husband could advance with his company. All major life changes in one swoop. I had a business degree but wanted to stay home with my newborn and work. I wanted my child to have a great home life I had pictured as a child. I dreamed of a life like those in The Brady Bunch and Leave It To Beaver. Those families gathered to talk instead of yell and they were happy.

I struggled through several more parties, reading from the script I was given. I had zero confidence. But I pressed forward, knowing I needed to make a certain income so I could stay home with my child. Oxytocin is the hormone that helps mothers love and do anything for their children. I had tons of it, and it took over. One day a time, one phone call at a time, pressing through the fear.

A turning point came when I secured a speaking event at a church women's club. My company sponsor would come with me and do all the talking, while I would help behind the scenes. Then an out-of-state family emergency took my sponsor away at the last minute. I said we should postpone the presentation until she returned to town, but she wouldn't hear it. She said I had to go on and do the presentation I had worked so hard to land. After all, I did have a script to follow.

It was a large group, perhaps twenty people. I had barely mastered talking in front of four or six people, but I had a feeling in my gut, an intuition that exciting things could come on the other side of that presentation, if only I could get through it.

Twice that week I went to the church hall where the women would gather for the presentation. I stood alone in that little cinder block room, shaking as I imagined 20 faces looking back at me. I practiced as if the seats were full.

The evening of the event, the club president was very curt and almost mean, not the same demeanor as when we set the date. I hadn't bargained for this, and I could feel the tears forming. But there was no time to cry; the meeting was beginning.

I turned off the lights and introduced myself in the dark from the back of the room. Their necks craned to see where the mystery voice was coming from. I started the slides and read from the script, almost robotic-sounding as the audience looked forward toward the slides. I spoke to the backs of their heads, a great opportunity to catch my breath. One woman heckled the entire time, but I came to find that there is one in almost every crowd. As kids they learned that if they weren't getting the attention they craved, they could get it through negative energy.

Then it was time to turn on the lights and take center stage—well, center cinder block in the front of the room. I became aware that this was the club president's first meeting. She herself was nervous and on edge. I brought her to the front of the room and lifted her up in front of her peers by thanking her for the great job and giving her a present. Everyone applauded her, and the attention shifted away from me.

Many women asked questions after my presentation and commented that they really liked the slides. When I arrived home that night, I was floating on air. My husband asked how much future business I had scheduled. Oops, bookings? My personal growth was so exciting I had forgotten the very thing I was there for.

I was still the worst recruiter ever, but eventually bookings and my first team member came from that group. It took twenty interviews, each one an hour, until the first person agreed to join. I still remember the happy dance I did in my kitchen.

Many obstacles later I stood on stage in front of an audience of nearly 5,000 as I was named Number 1 recruiter in the entire company. I maintained that title for years. As a fellow recruiter in my company back then, you would have watched me on our company training DVD. I also helped open our first international office and became corporate regional vice president, leading a team of over 13,000.

We start wherever we have to, but start we must. It's the act of beginning, when we are gripped with fear of the unknown, that the magic starts to seep out. Action alone activates our personal charisma. There is nothing quite like a person who has stepped out of her comfort zone repeatedly and is now living in the glory of her own 'it' factor. You can see it in the way she walks and talks. Each one of us must earn this for ourselves.

From the thousands I have worked with, it's apparent that self-confidence is an inside job that starts only with outside action. Jump in first, then get ready. Of course, we need a plan, but we cannot over-plan.

Running head first into your success provides an in-depth education that dotting the i's and crossing the t's can never match.

Taking action is the fastest learning curve. It affords real-life experiences that those waiting for the perfect time completely miss. The repetition of falling forward causes the fog to lift and the path to become clear. We have to step out of the shadows to feel the light on our face.

Go where you are celebrated, not where you are tolerated. There is a lifecycle in all goals. The first sign of a worthy goal is criticism, starting with your inner circle. Count on this with accuracy. That is the very first test of greatness that 97% don't pass. Expect it, for they cannot see what you see. Surround yourself with like-minded thinkers fast, before you start believing your great new find is crazy. Noise from the voices of many all singing the same song should not be allowed to drown out the one true voice, your own. At the end of our lives, it will be this voice that matters most.

ABOUT THE AUTHOR

Marybeth Rosato has over twenty-five years experience in leadership with proven results. She began as a struggling direct seller working through obstacles to become top seller, recruiter and leader year after year. Marybeth then became a corporate regional vice president in direct selling. She utilized her real life expertise to lead a sales force of thousands. Marybeth has been speaking and training all over the US and Canada helping audiences in her down to earth style, take action and find the courage to live 'on purpose'. Marybeth is a Direct Selling Women's Alliance Certified Coach, was instrumental in assisting to open an international market, is a founding board member and president of charity for women and children, and has served as a board member and volunteer at a leadership camp for youth.

Connect with Marybeth at:

www.linkedin.com/in/marybethrosato

ON THE COURT

By Terri Bork

n January 2008 my life changed forever. I lived a comfortable life in suburbia with my husband and two children in middle school. I did not need to worry about paying the bills because my husband made enough money for us all to live on. My job paid less than $700 a week before taxes. The money I earned paid for vacations, fun things for the family to do, and the kids' college education fund. I lived in a home with a mortgage of $2,200 a month, a car payment of $450, and an electric bill of $320. That January day, when he shut the door and left for the last time, I had no idea what I would do to support myself and my children, keep a roof over our heads, and put food on the table.

Corporate America and I did not always get along. I had many issues with being an employee in Corporate America, such as dictating when you can and cannot have time off. I had exhausted my vacation time with court dates and sick kids. They were not at all happy with my needing to take care of what needed to get done. I felt like I was in the stands, watching the game of my life being played out before me. I was miserable and felt trapped, I had no control in anything that was going on around me, worse yet, I did not know what to do to end the vicious cycle.

Even though I was in massive debt, I made the choice to leave my corporate job and work for myself. I would never let anyone decide what my income would be, when I could take a vacation, and what hours I was required to be on the job.

I started looking online but found nothing that worked to bring in extra money. I kept finding the wrong things and the wrong people to follow. I tried every multi-level marketing program I could find, spent money I did not have, and lost many friends with each scheme. I tried to make money by buying online courses that taught how to make money from home only to return the programs after 30 days to get my money back and pay for food. I was desperate. I felt like a miserable failure, and that feeling showed everywhere in my life.

Finally, after spending hours at the library, I learned how to make simple WordPress websites while I was in the process of my divorce. I had a few friends ask me to design websites for them, but my lawyer instructed me to wait until the divorce papers were signed or my ex-husband would get half of my earnings.

My divorce was final on March 4, 2009, a date that could not have had greater meaning for me. I could "MARCH FORTH" in my new life with my independence. On March 5, I filed for my LLC and Extreme Marketing Concepts was officially started! I did web-design and marketing for local brick and mortar businesses.

My small business soon grew as I started getting referrals to other small business. After several years, I hired a few people to perform the web design, marketing efforts, social media, and video marketing for our clients. Life was getting better, and I was playing on the court in my business.

After waiting six months for blog content from a client and at my wit's end, I decided to interview him. Not only did that interview give me tons of content for my client's blog, it spawned an entire new stream of business. I created a web TV show, Go Mind Your Business, and used it as a press conference for local businesses to share who they are, how they add value to their community, and why people should do business with them. As of the writing of this book, I have interviewed over 200 business owners and have added entrepreneurs and authors to my guest list.

James Allen writes in his book *As A Man Thinketh*, "Until thought is linked with purpose, there is no intelligent accomplishment." Unite your actions and thoughts to a specific purpose or defined goal to get the results you seek.

When I was starting out, I had to ask myself, "What do I really want to do with my life?" Most of us are visual. When we think about something we want, we see a picture of it in our minds. If I say think about your car, you immediately see your car in your mind. Visualization is very important. I wanted to make the six-figure income that I was comfortable with when my family was intact. For some people it is hard to say they want to make $100,000 a year when they are only making $25,000. How do you visualize that new amount of money in your mind? The process actually pretty simple. Break it down into smaller pieces:

Goal:	$100,000
Quarterly Goal:	$25,000
Monthly Goal:	$8,334
Weekly Goal:	$1,923
Daily Goal:	$274

All you need to do is focus on is today!

When my life changed that January morning, I was full of fear, regret, and indecision. Depressed and lifeless for a short time, I watched my life pass by and just cried. When I started to take action and learn web design, things started to turn around. I joined local networking organizations, met new people, and started getting referrals. I became empowered and finally took control of my life. I was able to choose the life I wanted for myself and my family. I let go of my limiting beliefs and found miracles.

Remember that everyone fails every once in awhile. I failed for many months and had debt of over $70,000. I had to get that debt under control. Between finding people to assist me with marketing local business owners to finding guests for my internet web TV show, I have started to get the debt under control. My kids are proud of me and encourage me daily to go for what I want in life.

My newest endeavor is coaching others to do what I do so they can create the life they want for themselves. Specifically, I want women to know that they do not have to depend on a spouse to get them through. You can be successful, and with the right teachers, you can achieve anything. It is my honor to contribute to the success of others.

I want to leave you with this: You can make money doing anything. Everything that you are passionate about has the ability to generate money. Get out there, on the court, and find a way to create an income doing something you love. I am living a life I love and you can do the same. I used to think of my life as ordinary; now I see my life as extraordinary and the people I get to work with are up to great things. Here is to your massive success.

ABOUT THE AUTHOR

Terri Bork is an Author, Broadcaster, CEO, Speaker and mother of two. She is passionate about helping her clients grow their business and make the money they deserve. Whether it be business owners looking to get the word out about their business and how they help others in the community or entrepreneurs who are looking to create a second source of income. Terri knows that you are extra-ordinary and loves being a contribution.

Find out more about Terri at <u>GoMindYourBusiness.com</u>

Connect with Terri at:

<u>www.facebook.com/terri.bork</u>

<u>twitter.com/TerriBork</u>

<u>www.linkedin.com/in/terribork/</u>

<u>www.google.com/+TerriBork</u>

THE PERFECT MATCH

By Lizette LaForge

H ave you ever had one of those life-changing moments when something so startling occurs that you forever remember where you were and how you felt on that day?

For me the day began innocently enough. It was a busy Friday in October 2009, and I was working hard on my new window and door replacement business. I was proud to have attained my contractor's license. That afternoon I was scheduled to attend a two-hour training course on how to network at business mixers. I felt like I didn't need the class—when I was born, the doctor slapped me and the networking began. Nonetheless, I went determined to learn what I could to help grow my budding business. I had no idea then how much the class would change my life.

In two short hours the instructor covered the ways people of different personality types engage in social and networking settings. Hours later, meditating on this information while shopping, a bolt of lightning seemed to course through my veins. I realized I was not fully utilizing my personality in my business life. I am an extreme extrovert intent on getting results. From that day forward I have thought long and hard about how to come into my purpose.

My passion in life revolves around assisting people who are on the path to helping others, by providing them connections that help them accomplish their goals. It became clear to me that I experience intense satisfaction from connecting people to their perfect matches, particularly with regard to business interests. In effect, my business is all about you!

I came to realize that helping others with higher-purpose goals would allow me the opportunity to dynamically change the world for the better. As this understanding unfolded and blended with desire, I became a Joint Venture Facilitator, branding myself "the Queen of the In-Between!" In that capacity, I analyze people and products strategically and then connect them to others to their mutual business benefit.

To illustrate: Like a bee, I pollinate. I do not use just any pollen, however, but the correct pollen to make the joint venture a success. If you are a papaya, then as the bee I need to bring you papaya pollen. I can't bring pineapple pollen and expect a fruitful result just because both live in tropical climates and look great together in a fruit salad. In this same fashion, by understanding my clients' needs and bringing them the correct solutions, we get the desired results.

To do this I listen intently to my clients and examine them like a jeweler examines a fine diamond—carefully scrutinizing each facet. This involves understanding their history, goals, and intentions—really anything that will help me get a comprehensive awareness of their needs. Where is the client in their business and their life, and where would they like to go? What do they need to attain those goals?

This higher level overview lets me see what puzzle pieces they may need to create or add to their success. This examination also allows me to see if they are a puzzle piece for others.

By taking such an intense look, I know what pollen to provide them. I then work strategically to showcase their beautiful diamond-like facets to others and close business, resulting in a win-win situation for all. This is known as a Joint Venture or JV.

What types of things do I look for? I love technical tools and teams, products, programs, or people that help get things done faster or more efficiently, especially on the Internet. People who help others, whether in business, real estate, or health are another favorite.

I'll describe a few examples to give you an idea of the many businesses that can be JV'd. Recently I developed a deal for a local radio personality who specializes in real estate and business to reach a national audience. I am helping him connect to a company that helps people buy and flip businesses like others buy and flip houses, but much more profitably. That training will resonate with his audience and help them succeed.

I am also helping a husband and wife doctor team develop a team of health and wellness professionals and programs with offerings that will truly benefit people. A client to whom I am connecting them developed protocols that remediate the debilitating effects of multiple sclerosis. By connecting these two powerful teams, we can get that life-changing message out to many more people.

In the Internet marketing arena, I have clients who are looking for cutting edge, effective programs to offer their customer lists and other clients who create these programs to distribute to customer lists. For example, one of my clients offers a very easy-to-follow tablet computer course that allows businesses to create and post professional-looking videos in just a few minutes. I am bringing his offer to other Internet Marketers whose customers are small businesses.

Think of a peanut butter and jelly sandwich. Once upon a time, someone introduced the two ingredients. But first, many people played a role in developing the sandwich. Someone bought the land and someone planted the peanuts and fruit. They also had to be harvested, processed, manufactured, shipped, and then assembled into a sandwich. When you think of all the people and businesses that had a hand in creating such a simple snack, you realize there can easily be well over 100 joint ventures just in the PB&J example. Extrapolate those lessons into your life and business, and let the magic begin!

With JVs, my business is all about your business. To really show you what I do, we need to make this personal and see how you might use joint ventures in your business.

So, what do you do? Let's examine your diamond. Tell me a little about your history and how it has gotten you to where you are today. What is your industry? Are you a speaker, author, or coach? How do you, your programs, or your products help others? Do you promote your business through Google Hangouts? Who are your targets, and how do you connect with them? Remember to be specific. Use sniper-rifle focus rather than a buckshot approach to achieve better results.

Have you examined cross-selling opportunities into other industries and with other vendors who don't compete with you? Yes. We're talking JVs here!

What are your goals for yourself and your business? JVs are not always related to business interests, so keep that in mind as you explore the concept. Regarding resources, what do you have to offer others and what do you need for greater success?

I enjoy helping people by offering a one-hour strategy session to explore how joint ventures might work for you in reaching your business and life goals.

ABOUT THE AUTHOR

Born and raised in Massachusetts, Lizette and her family now reside in sunny St Petersburg Florida, home of the newly wed or nearly dead. She enjoys cooking and outdoor activities such as camping and gardening.

As a Joint Venture Facilitators, Lizette and her partner Torsten Nielsen connect clients to their perfect business matches. By using intensive listening strategies, Lizette has an uncanny ability to "see" synergies between people and products.

Puzzled on how to grow your business? Let Lizette and Torsten find the perfect pieces to your success! Schedule your appointment with Lizette LaForge, the Queen of the In-Between, at www.YourJVMatchmaker.com.

Connect with Lizette at:

facebook.com/yourjvmatchmaker

twitter.com/jvmatchmaker

www.linkedin.com/company/yourjvmatchmaker

THE CIRCUS WITHIN

By Nancy S. Davies

'm first generation circus. The circus and I met early in my life, and it later blossomed into a life-long friend and combatant. It made me happy but it also broke my heart; it gave me direction. I pursued my circus dream, turning it into reality, until that dream turned into a nightmare. Nobody tells you what to do if that happens.

"No, it's dirty in there," said my mother when I asked to go into the circus one evening when I was nine years old. The show had set up its tent in an open field at the end of our street. My mother's response confused me since it had been her idea to walk there after dinner. I heard music and the sounds of the elephants, but I couldn't see them due to the canvas walls they'd erected around the midway. All I could see was the entrance and top of the tent. As people paid their money and disappeared inside, I stood there, disappointed, until my mother took my hand and we headed home, the music fading. Ten years later an amusement park summer job had me working with a circus. I was hooked.

Many years passed before mom accepted my passion for the circus. She was fearful I'd run away and join a show, which I almost did during my college years. She still wasn't thrilled when, in my 20s, I created the opportunity to become a part-time circus ringmaster. Her acceptance finally began in my 30s when I applied to work for a public relations agency that represented a circus. It became my account when I was hired. Though working with this circus had some difficulties, the many more joyous moments made me happy. In my 40s I felt the now-or-never drive to pursue my lifelong dream of being on the road with a circus. Setting a deadline of one year, it was nearly a year to the day that the Big Apple Circus hired me as their company manager. I accepted a salary far less than I'd been making, and so began the teachings of the circus.

Lesson #1: The circus doesn't pay well; figure out your new life finances.

I gave notice at work, sold my car, purchased an RV and one-ton pick-up truck to pull it, packed, stored my belongings, then put my condominium up for sale. Two weeks after my 43rd birthday, feeling elated and fearful, I carefully drove my truck with RV in tow from Chicago to Boston to join the show and my new reality.

This wasn't just a job I was going to; it was a way of life, and not one for the faint of heart. Was I ready for the long hours, hard work, six- and seven-day workweeks, inconveniences, excessive travel, frozen water lines, vehicle breakdowns, and unforeseen unpleasant tasks? When instructed to dump the RV toilets from departing performers' trailers, I wondered. When broken lines ran sewage over my hands, I questioned.

But, Lesson #2: Life is messy, and one unpleasant task doesn't define the choices we make.

The circus is a close-knit community. Some are born into it and others, like me, choose it. Before I joined the show, friends and family were mostly supportive, though some said, "I wouldn't do it, but it's good you are pursuing your dream." Others exclaimed, "Don't do it; what if you hate it?" My response was always, "What if I love it?" To my shock, it turned out to be both, but I've never regretted it.

Lesson #3: Because I thoughtfully took the leap, I will never have to wonder, "What if?"

My new life was good but the job itself was often surprisingly boring. Then unexpectedly, nearly a year after I'd started out on this dream adventure, the "big show" I'd interviewed with nearly two years prior called and offered me an interesting position. Weighing the pros and cons, I became an assistant production manager with the most well known circus in the United States. I couldn't foresee that soon my circus career would be at an end.

Lesson #4: Life is full of surprises.

The new circus insisted I was needed immediately, which meant I had to temporarily leave behind my home and vehicle until my now former employer finished its run in New York City and the RVs could be moved. With only a suitcase of clothes, I flew to Florida. Arriving at 9 p.m., waiting patiently for the promised airport pick-up to take me to my new home on a train—another adventure—I wondered why I was the only one left at baggage claim.

More than an hour later and with my calls going directly to voicemail, I checked into the airport hotel and waited. And waited some more. It wasn't until 3 p.m. the next day that my messages were returned. With no apology, just the excuse they'd forgotten I was arriving, I was picked up an hour later and things went downhill from there.

Lesson #5: When those insisting you are needed immediately forget about you, it's a sign of worse things to come.

I was taken directly to the show arena and the bullying by my direct supervisor began. She didn't want me there, that was clear. Toward me she was unpleasant, insulting, and condescending on the rare occasions she deigned to speak to me, while also being obstructive and petty. Everything was designed to force me to quit, including requiring I needlessly be at the arena for 17 hours every day of our regular six-day workweeks. The lonely, worsening nightmare included snubbing and cattiness by some performers and crew members who had been told stories about me. These were the very people I needed to build trust and respect with in order to do my job. When there was no relief after speaking with management, I became depressed and silently angry. After all, everything I'd worked for and sacrificed in order to pursue my lifelong dream was now meaningless because the circus had become toxic. After careful consideration, and confirmation from a trusted, long-time show insider that things would only continue to deteriorate, I knew it was time to go. I resigned after a measly two weeks.

Lesson #6: Nothing is worth the cost of your well-being.

Being professional, I gave the show two weeks' notice so my time with them stretched to one month. That may not seem like much but I discovered it far exceeded the two days my predecessor had worked.

For a year I was sad, embarrassed, and bitter by this loss. No one understood, and I was judged. Many said to me, "You didn't give it a chance; you gave up too easily." But they didn't live it. Only I knew its ugliness and, without a doubt, I had made the correct, albeit, painful choice.

Lesson #7: Don't carry the judgments of those who don't know.

Each day, ever so slowly, the hurt lessened until I was able to regain control and move forward to realize new dreams. But first I needed to let my love, and hurt, of the circus go.

Lesson #8: Let go of pain to make room for the positive.

And Lesson #9: Every choice we make puts us on a path. If we don't like the path, we can choose a different direction. I chose the circus, then I chose to leave it. Both of those decisions helped lead me to the man I was to marry. Later, I started my own circus-themed company. It turns out the circus never left me; it can't. It's woven into the fabric of my being.

The oft-quoted saying, "Life is a circus," is true; I've lived it, but I also add, "Be the ringmaster." Take charge and direct your life to your satisfaction. If you can add sequins to it, all the better! My nine-year-old self may not have been allowed to enter the circus, but my young imagination kept the dream safely tucked away until I could afford my own ticket.

Lesson #10: Whether we take a leap of faith, clown around, or juggle tasks, the circus lives within us all.

Full disclosure: There was one lesson I didn't learn when I was with the circus: how to back up my RV. It's difficult. I wish I had.

As this chapter ends my journey continues. It is my hope our paths will cross again so I may one day have the honor to hear your story. Until such time, as we say in the circus, I'll see you down the road.

ABOUT THE AUTHOR

 Nancy S. Davies is a Circuspirational Speaker, Author, Coach and the owner of www.BeTheRingmaster.com, a company designed to inspire & help guide those who wish to manifest their dreams and goals while thoughtfully directing the three ring circus of their lives. Her insights come from working with six different U.S. circuses, as well as personal experience of creating and making her own dreams come true. In addition, Nancy is an accomplished Publicist, Media Trainer, Actor, Voice-Over Talent and former award-winning Television Producer. Additional information about her can be found at www.NancyDaviesOnline.com.

Twitter.com/circusgirl

www.facebook.com/BeTheRingmaster.com.

HOW AMBITION, DETERMINATION AND EFFORT GIVE YOU THE RESOURCES AND SECURITY TO SERVE OTHERS

By Regina Smola

J ane Addams said, "The good we secure for ourselves is precarious and uncertain until it is secured for all of us and incorporated into our common life."

This reminds me of my childhood, trying to understand how to make sense of circumstances and situations out of my control. I wondered what I could do to make things better or to help secure a safe haven for my family and me. What I learned was powerful and effective!

As an adolescent there were certain things I wanted, such as a Yorkie puppy. When I told my mother this, she said it was fine but I had to work for it. At age twelve I knew I needed to find a way to make this dream come true, so I took on both paper routes in our small town. At age fourteen I started working at the local ice cream shop as well. The hard work paid off when I secured my sweet dog, Bo. I am grateful to my mother for instilling in me the importance of turning my dreams into reality by planning and working for them.

My parents could not afford to pay for my college, so I enrolled in a legal secretary training program while still in high school. I graduated when I was seventeen, and shortly after I got my first full-time job as a legal secretary. At night I worked a second job at a car dealership.

As my skills expanded and I desired to do more with my life, I took State tests that led to jobs with the Department of Revenue and the Department of Corrections. Through ambition and determination I was climbing the corporate ladder.

But I became discouraged as I watched others take credit and money for the work I had done. I knew I needed to search for my purpose in life and fulfill the passions that burned in my soul.

Then my life took on a new challenge—one that I embraced. I got married and was blessed with two wonderful boys. Unfortunately, it didn't take long to learn that even the security of marriage can be disrupted. My boys mean everything to me. Their well-being and hope for a future became solely my responsibility as a single parent.

I worked two and three jobs at a time. I struggled to make ends meet and felt guilty for not being a full-time mom. To spend more time with my kids, I quit my "real" job and decided to work from home. I started my own company in women's shooting sports that produced promotional materials and an online forum. We traveled across the country to various sports stores, hunting clubs, radio shows, and commercials. This led to an offer for a television show.

I've always had an entrepreneurial spirit. When I was young, I used my allowance to buy a baby food jar, nail polish remover, and a sponge. I cleaned the jar, cut the sponge to fit inside, and put a slice down the middle. Then I filled it with nail polish remover, screwed the lid on, and hot-glued a pretty ribbon on top. It was a Mother's Day gift for my mom. I showed my friends, and they all wanted to make one for their moms. Something similar showed up on store shelves a year or so later.

In 2000, I woke up and couldn't feel my legs from the waist down. I spent several weeks in the hospital. After being poked and prodded, I was diagnosed with Chronic Inflammatory Demyelinating Polyneuropathy. The feeling in my legs came back eventually, but there is no cure, and I still experience nerve pain, weakness, and numbness from time to time. Rather than take dangerous steroids or treatments, I have learned to just live with the disease. My business traveling days were over, though, and I closed my business down.

In 2004, my mom and I began an affiliate website promoting merchant coupons. We took out a startup loan and paid a developer $3,000 to create a custom PHP website for us. We were excited to have an income stream working from our homes.

Shortly after the site was launched, however, it was hacked. The hosting company technician told me we needed to clean it. It took me over three weeks to manually remove all the malicious code on over 3,000 files. I sure wish I had known about backups back then.

About six months later our site was hacked again. The hosting company technician asked, "Did you change your password?" I said, "Well, no, you didn't tell me I needed to." I wanted to kick myself for not thinking of it. I had to clean the website again (and change our passwords). I also decided to learn everything I could to keep hackers off our website.

The coupon site was a very competitive field, and my mom and I got little return on our investment, so we decided to close it down. I took on a few retainer clients to work from home, building, securing, and maintaining their WordPress websites. When they made money selling their digital products, I thought, Wow! I wish I could do that! I also got referrals to clean other hacked websites. Helping them clean and secure their sites was very gratifying for me.

My friend Kelli Claypool asked me to speak at a teleseminar for her online community about website security. During the event, questions poured in and there was a huge interest in what I had to say. Afterward, I received thank you emails with even more questions on web site security. I was ready to use my knowledge to help others.

In 2010, I started my own services business helping people secure their WordPress websites and restore sites that were hacked. It was an untapped market that began to draw a population of people in need. I knew it was my opportunity to fulfill my purpose with passion.

In an effort to take my business to the next level, I decided to attend the Novice to Advanced Marketing System (NAMS) Conference in Atlanta in August 2010. This became another opportunity to use my efforts and resources to serve others. There is great value in taking the time to learn from others, build relationships, and apply what I have learned. David Perdew, the founder of NAMS, recognized my desire and ability to serve others in a productive way and continues to mentor me. He has given me the platform to share my knowledge and help many as a NAMS Instructor.

My hope in sharing my story is to encourage you to find your purpose in life, whether personal or professional. If I can do it, you can too! It takes effort and determination, but you can be empowered with confidence, security, and resources. You are unique and have much to offer others.

I am reminded that no experience, good or bad, is wasted. By observing what we have learned and thinking back to what was, we gain the courage to soldier on, knowing that nothing happens by accident. It is for our good and for the good of others.

My passion is to teach others how to stay safe online, to keep their sites more secure, and to fix sites that fall victim to hacker attacks. Some quick tips on how to help keep your web site safe from hackers:

- Keep your computer up-to-date, stay behind a firewall, run anti-virus software 24/7, avoid non-secured Wi-Fi, and perform backups and store them securely (online or external HD).
- Use a strong and unique password for every online account (18+ characters with a combination of upper and lower case letters, numbers, and symbols).
- Use a reliable and trustworthy hosting company.
- Schedule frequent website backups (files and databases) and store securely offsite.

- Update your WordPress (or CMS) core files, plugins, and themes regularly.
- Ensure that your team/staff are following the same security practices.

Securely yours.

Regina Smola

ABOUT THE AUTHOR

Regina Smola has been an entrepreneur since 1999 and became a victim of a compromised website in 2004. She then began her journey to build her knowledge of website and online security. Through her passion and motivation, Regina is a sought-after security expert. She has helped thousands of WordPress users tighten security on their blogs and cleaned hundreds of malware-infected websites. Her security advice has also been featured on Entrepreneur.com.

Whether working one-on-one with clients, as a team facilitator, security service provider or an inspiring speaker, Regina's commitment to website owners about the dangers and behaviors of malicious hackers is second to none.

If you would like to learn more about securing your website or need help getting your website fixed, visit Regina's website at wpsecuritylock. com or email support@wpsecuritylock.com.

www.facebook.com/wpsecuritylock
www.twitter.com/wpsecuritylock
plus.google.com/+Wpsecuritylock
www.linkedin.com/in/reginasmola

TREASURE YOUR LIFE NOW

By Sheila Finkelstein

"What's a piece of cardboard?" I wrote in a poem. I listed a multitude of things, and continued with, "You may make discoveries as yet unknown. I am not the possessor of all knowledge, all ideas. I can be the source from which you can get help to develop your own ideas, your individuality, your uniqueness…What's a feather, a piece of cloth, a strange shape, a can of nails, a box of scrap wood? That's up to you, my dear friend…Up to you to collage your life a rich and vibrant one."

As I read those words thirty-seven years after I wrote them, I see how much they express the core of who I am and my commitment to individuals of any age recognizing and developing their own creativity and strengths.

The selection is from "ODE TO A PIECE OF CARDBOARD — Philosophy of Art Education and Life," written in 1977. (See TreasureYourLifeNow.com/ode for the complete poem). It is a compilation of phrases I jotted down at every red light on my way to a class at Rutgers University Graduate School of Education.

I was expelling my anger at the principal of the elementary school where I taught art from a traveling cart. As I headed out the door one afternoon, she commented, "A bomb could go off in your closet and no one would be any the worse for it!"

The closet she referred to was the one that housed the school supplies, plus my cart and materials. I offered a wide range of visual and sensory experiences for the students, and my somewhat non-traditional organization didn't fit her sense of order.

Writing in the moment is a most effective release for me and one I recommend to clients when it fits. By the time I got to class, my anger was gone. When I got home I formed my scattered words into the poem, typed it, and placed it on the principal's desk the next morning.

The results of my approach are evident in an email I received from Linda Bailey Walsh, one of my students at that time. She found me on the web thirty-five years later. Now an actress, writer, comedian, and make-up artist in Los Angeles, Linda wrote, "Someone asked me to recall the first person who truly inspired me artistically, and it was you." She went on to fill me in on her life and mentioned that she had been going through her yearbook and had read what I wrote.

She continued, "Wow. I wonder if you can understand how much that meant to me in sixth grade and seeing it again tonight so many years later? You let me know I was seen, and that was an enormous thing for me."

As I reflect on Linda's words, I'm reminded of my own experiences of being seen and the impact it has had on me, as well as the ripple effect on all those for whom my teaching, coaching, and photography has made a difference.

For this I acknowledge my beloved husband Sam, who died in 2007. During my first twenty years of life, my parents planted the seeds for my interest in nature, leadership, curiosity, and a love for helping people. Then I met and fell in love with Sam. He fostered my creative birth—the opportunity to develop and expand into what became my passion for discovery and sharing with others.

Most importantly, Sam's unconditional love provided space for my self-esteem to develop and grow. Very often we are challenged in loving ourselves. At times we need reminders. The emotional security Sam gave me became the underlying foundation for most of the work I've done during these past fifty years. No matter what the business, the core was and is believing in yourself and seeing your own greatness.

This thread wove its way through my teaching art to elementary and high school students many years ago, then into several successful sales positions, where service and communication were fundamental. Ten years ago I launched *Picture to Ponder* e-zine with my inspirational photography and "self-reflecting queries." From that came many Photography as Access to Seeing workshops and teleseminars, then relationship coaching. Now the access to connecting and communicating with yourself and your loved ones is the foundation of Technology for Seniors Made Easy, a business that evolved from my story with Sam.

Sam and I were engaged six weeks after we met and married three months later. I was finishing my junior year in college in Philadelphia, our home city. He was working in New York. Given the prohibitive cost of long-distance phone calls at the time, he would write almost daily between weekend visits. I am blessed to still have most of those letters, plus other notes over the next forty-seven years, all with beautiful expressions of his feelings.

A week after Sam died, just when I needed it the most, a message of love, with beautifully reinforcing supportive words, surfaced on my desk. His words described my strengths from his perspective, enough to help me pull forward, walking into his image of me, honoring him by honoring myself and not staying immersed in grief.

Though grateful that I had his letters and cards, I began to regret not having the sound of his voice. I certainly had all the skills and experience to have done quick recordings and simple videos. The importance of doing this had never occurred to me. I realized that many people might not even have letters from a loved one who's passed, and coupled with missing Sam's voice, I was compelled to launch my Love With No Regrets coaching practice.

Technology for Seniors Made Easy evolved to support seniors to confidently use technology to capture memories and communicate and connect with their family and friends, as well as to find information and things most important to them.

In addition to our beliefs in ourselves, flexibility and resilience are two other main factors that make our lives run smoothly. An example of this in my own life follows. Relocating to New York after we were married, I left college at the end my third year. I returned to another university eight years later, where I changed my major from Sociology to Fine Arts Education.

At the end of "Painting and Drawing," my first course in the major, my instructor told me to "drop out of school and join a local art guild to satisfy [my] housewifely ambitions." Though I felt her harsh words in my gut, I did not follow her "advice." Six months later I was back. My self-image had grown strong enough for me to stand in my belief that one did not need to be a great artist to be a good teacher. I excelled in all the other art courses I took and was fortunate to get a full-time teaching position in my hometown.

I used my first paycheck to buy a second Pentax camera. Sam's avocation was photography and he did beautiful work. While traveling we would take pictures of what caught our eyes. Often the subject would be the same yet we each would view it from a slightly different perspective. For the most part, I used the camera to document my students working and their finished projects. Sam, in support of me, spent late hours developing and printing countless pictures. Several of the photos ended up in national publications.

After five years in the district, despite the public protest of parents and teachers, my art position was eliminated due to decline in enrollment.

I moved on to being trained as an outside salesperson, attaining "Salesperson of the Month" in a national company in one of the first months I was there. Over time I moved on to several different sales jobs, always pulled by new discoveries, consistently drawn to providing service. Ultimately, I began to focus on creating my own business.

My innovative photo/drawings led to Nature's Playground and my first website. When Sam and I moved to Florida, one of our Pentax cameras was retired for a digital camera. I started taking countless photographs of the natural wonders in our new surrounding. Ultimately I learned just enough computer and photo processing skills to share my work online, and during later telecourses, my students shared their work as well. As I toured my environments with the camera, participants toured theirs. In addition to increasing their self-confidence, enhancing relationships, and expanding creativity, some developed new businesses or strengthened existing ones.

Ten years before his death, Sam was diagnosed with Parkinson's Disease. Thus, caregiver became one more role in my life. I experienced the importance of being and staying connected with others. Although PD had its debilitating effects on him, Sam remained strong both mentally and emotionally. His biggest concern was for me.

In summation, referencing the poem with which I started, if you need help believing in yourself, developing your creative self-expression, living a life with no regrets, or using technology to experience the rewards and joy of connecting and communicating with loved ones and the world, simply contact me. And be sure to download *Treasure Your Life Now—How to Be in the Moment.*

ABOUT THE AUTHOR

Sheila Finkelstein, "The Tech Savvy Senior", has also been referred to as "The Lens to Life Discovery." With a wide range of life and business experiences, she has incorporated her three main businesses and passions into TREASURE YOUR LIFE NOW. This encompasses the work reflected on <u>PhotographyandTransformation.com</u>, <u>LovewithNoRegrets.com</u> and <u>TechnologyforSeniorsMadeEasy.com</u>.

Family and communication are those areas most vital, given her 47-year love-filled marriage with two sons, their wives, and four grandchildren.

Throughout whatever path she pursued, her prime motivation has been to support students and clients in believing in themselves, always seeing possibility. The technology business supports this, teaching the how-to's of easily, communicating with family and friends worldwide. In 2013, Women in Ecommerce presented Sheila with the annual Golden Mouse Lifetime Achievement award. See TreasureYourLifeNow. com for more information and tips.

Connect with Sheila at:

www.facebook.com/sheilafinkelstein

twitter.com/InspiredSheila

twitter.com/TechSavvySr

www.linkedin.com/in/sheilafinkelstein

plus.google.com/u/0/110254057431738742639/

NEVER SAY NEVER

By Deanna Gillingham

had been a nurse for well over 10 years, but it was my first day to scrub into surgery without my preceptor. I had that nervous excitement you get when something you have been working hard for is finally about to happen. A year before I had said I would never scrub into surgery, and now I was excited about it.

When Grace walked into the room, I knew instantly that something was wrong by the downward cast of her eyes and solemn look on her face. She began by telling me I did not have to scrub in, and that no one would be upset with me if I refused, but there had been a change of plans.

Normally for your first solo scrub-in, you are paired with a mellow surgeon, someone laid-back. That was the plan for me, but the plan had changed. I was needed to scrub in with Dr. B. Now I was not a new nurse, just new to the operating room. I had been around long enough to hear the stories about Dr. B screaming at nurses in the Operating Room and throwing instruments across the room. There wasn't much time to think about it. The patient was being wheeled into the OR. If I would not do the case, staffing changes would need to be made to the entire unit.

As Dr. B walked into the OR, I could feel my anxiety mounting. This was it. I humbly explained, "This is my first solo scrub in. If you want someone more experienced, I understand, but I'm really excited to be learning from you. Just tell me what you want me to do." Then I held my breath and waited for the verbal assault. "Well good, I'll get to train you the right way," he said, with what I'm sure was a smile under his surgical mask.

Dr. B took on the role of teacher and I the excited student. My nervousness left, and I was caught up in the wonder and awe of delivering a baby by caesarean section. It is stressful from the first cut until the baby is delivered and handed to the nursery nurse. After that, the atmosphere is more relaxed, and I began to really get into the surgery. I was so into it that at one point Dr. B asked me if I could see well. I thought it was so kind of him to ask. "Yes, I can see just fine," I replied. "I know," he responded, "because I can't see a damn thing." He began laughing and informed me it was a common mistake for newbies. He then instructed me to hold the instruments so he could also see and put everything back where it was supposed to be.

After this, I began to see challenges as opportunities. Instead of resisting, I welcomed them as a chance to grow. A few years later, I found myself again doing something I said I would never do: leave direct patient care for a desk job. After nearly twenty years working as a bedside nurse, an injury was making it impossible to spend twelve hours on my feet, as bedside nursing required. Even a four-hour shift was difficult. A friend had been trying to convince me to take a desk job at an insurance company, and eventually it became apparent that the decision was being made for me.

As I walked out of the hospital for the last time that warm spring day, the mixture of emotions was overwhelming. I was wavering between contentment, grief, excitement, and worry. As I looked back on my career, I realized I had done everything I had hoped to when I began the journey many years before. I had comforted patients experiencing life-threatening illness. I was there when newborn babies took their first breath. I cared for patients who were teetering between life and death, stabilized them, and nursed them back to health. And when nothing else could be done, I held their hands as they departed this earthly life.

I was grieving the fact that I would no longer be doing this fulfilling work. On the other hand, I was excited that for the first time in my career, I would work a 40-hour week—no nights, weekends, holidays, or on-call shifts. I would be able to work from my home, making it easier to handle the dual roles of mother and nurse. I worried, though, that I would not be able to make a difference in the lives of others.

The Case Management position turned out to be the perfect position for me. I could use my knowledge and expertise to make a difference in the lives of many others.

One such person was Mr. G. He had been hospitalized for over three months at a major medical center two hours from his home, creating tremendous hardship for his family. His children were in school, and his wife had returned to work to keep their health benefits as well as their income. He wasn't able to see his family often and was becoming depressed as a result. After talking with the hospital staff and his wife, it became evident to me that the depression was taking a toll on this health. We feared that if we did not move him closer to home and family, he would stop fighting.

We made the decision to transfer him closer to home, but to do this was more difficult than expected. After weeks of phone calls, planning, and negotiations, a week before Thanksgiving everyone agreed we had exhausted every means, and it just wasn't going to happen. I prayed, asking God to take over and perform a miracle, and then I set it aside.

Over a month later, just days before Christmas, I was wrapping up my work in preparation to take time off for the holidays. The phone rang; it was the facility in Mr. G's hometown where we had been trying to transfer him. They wanted to transfer him to their facility on Monday. Once again, the phone calls, negations, and planning began. This time everything went smoothly. What I could not do in weeks before was done in a few hours. It was a Christmas miracle, and on December 23, he arrived in his hometown and spent Christmas with his family.

Within three weeks of arriving in his hometown, he was well enough to go home.

Then I found myself doing something else I said I would never do again: taking a certification exam. I had become certified in oncology nursing many years before and found the process extremely stressful. I vowed to never take another certification exam. But if I wanted to keep my job working from home, I would have to become certified in Case Management.

I became frustrated searching for materials to help me study for the exam. I couldn't find exactly what I was looking for, so I decided to create it. At the same time I began diligently networking, creating online study sessions, and a website to help other nurses study with me. As a response to a real need in my life, I created a full-fledged online business and helped others reach their goals.

ABOUT THE AUTHOR

Deanna Gillingham is a Registered Nurse, online entrepreneur and mother to four children and two fur babies. Her twenty years of nursing experience include Med/Surg, ICU, LDRP, OR, Oncology, Outpatient Clinics, Home Health, Hospice and Case Management. Her love for her profession combined with her passion for helping others led to her creation of www. TheStayAtHomeNurse.com and www.CaseManagementStudyGuide. com to assist nurses in reaching their career and life goals.

Connect with Deanna at:

facebook.com/TheStayAtHomeNurse

twitter.com/StayAtHomeNurse

www.linkedin.com/in/deannagillingham/

plus.google.comu/

/b/103425970606447384621/103425970606447384621/

about/p/pub

THE PERFECT SALES STORM

By Steve Rosenbaum

I will never forget the date. July 19, 1989.

That day I began my quest to help businesses and people close more sales and make more money. To learn what I learned, and to experience what I experienced. It was the beginning of my metamorphosis into "The Original Back End Specialist."

I was a newly-hired, eager-to-succeed ball of fire. I was given a territory of my own for the first time, and I was out to prove myself come hell or high water. So I attacked the account list with great vigor and made a six-hour trek to call on an eighteen-location department store in Quincy, Illinois.

Peggy, the buyer, was very nice when I called to set the appointment. "You know, it would be nice to meet you, but Quincy is a long way for you," she told me on the phone. "I hate for you to make the trip because your chances of succeeding are almost nil. We're exclusive with the number one brand, and I don't see that changing anytime soon."

Now what kind of Territory Manager would I be if let a 700-mile round-trip journey keep me from checking an account off of my list? I thought to myself. Of course I would make the trip.

When I arrived, Peggy was nice as could be and escorted me to her office. After the normal greetings and formalities, I began my pitch, demonstrating the luggage. I showed her all the bells and whistles, opened and closed the zippers, spun the wheels, and extended and collapsed the handles.

In my mind, I did all this with flawless expertise and perfection. Obviously I possessed skills and talent that surpassed anything she had ever seen before. In reality, of course, I simply did the exact same things that every other luggage schlepper in the history of the universe did.

In teaching my students a better way to market and sell, I've developed a technical term to describe what happens when a salesperson engages in this kind of one-sided exhibition: It's called a "Show Up and Throw Up."

And then, the phone rang. This was before the days of call screening. Ring-ring, ring-ring. "Excuse me. Let me see who it is," Peggy apologized. "Of course," I replied sweetly, masking my deep irritation and annoyance.

She picked up the phone and I heard her side of the conversation: "Oh, I see. Well, that's not good…Ouch, that's really, really going to be a problem for me…There's nothing you can do? Oh, my goodness… I'm really in big trouble…OK, well I really have to go," she said as she returned the handset to the cradle.

With that she turned to me and said, "Well, that was your number one competitor, the one that I said you would never unseat. They called to inform me that my shipping container of luggage for an ad in two weeks is held up in Customs and is not going to get here in time. I'm not going to have the luggage I need for the ad. So I need to know right now what you have at this price point that we could run in its place."

I excused myself and used a phone in the next office to call my boss, the vice president of sales. He was ecstatic, to say the least. This was a target account that they had been trying to crack for years. We had suitable inventory, and I closed the deal! She wrote a tremendous order, somewhere near $50,000. That was a very big order for us.

My company thought I was a rock star. Like me, they were convinced that I was absolutely the most brilliant salesman in the history of selling luggage.

That sale started my trajectory into sales management. Two months later the company moved my family to California and made me the Western Regional Sales Manager. A year and a half later, at 28 years old, another company recruited me away and gave me a VP of Sales position in Savannah, Georgia. It all began with that one sale.

Sales success came easy, at first. Later, I discovered that sales didn't always come that easy. Reality set in, and I learned that just showing up didn't always make it happen. I found out that even if I made a perfect, flawless pitch, I didn't always get the sale.

I returned in my mind to Quincy and dissected the situation over and over again. What really happened? The phone call is what happened. Peggy was in need. She turned to the easiest and best solution she could find that happened to be sitting eighteen inches away from her, and asked, "Can you cure my pain?" And she gave me the opportunity.

A lot of things came together at the same time and created the perfect storm for me. I was in the right place at the right time. I had the right message (that is, I had luggage that she needed), and I was in the right market (she was the luggage buyer).

Right place, right time, right message, right market. All four of those factors must be present to create a buyer who is ready, willing, and able to buy from you right now.

That was the lesson I learned. You might say, "You did a great job because you showed up." That is true. I made the trip. I was there. I made the presentation. I was able to take care of her needs. So, yes, I did execute the mechanics.

The point is, even if you do all the right things, but you're not in the right place, at the right time, in the right market, with the right message, you aren't going to get the sale.

How many times have you tried to make a sale, and someone said, "Call me back in six months. I'll be ready then." You diligently mark the date on your calendar and call back in six months. The same person says, "Darn, I wish you had called last week because the other guy called me and I gave the business to him." As a salesman and a business owner, I've been there. I'm sure you've been there too.

The Quincy experience was not lost on me. I set out to perfect a system where I could put the odds of bringing all four elements together in my favor.

It was the impetus for what I've honed and developed over the course of nearly twenty-five years. It's the back end of the marketing funnel, the follow-up process that happens after a person meets the business for the first time. It's also the part that most businesses fail to properly execute and results in a great deal of missed opportunity.

I've detailed my system in my book *Back End Blueprint*. I've broken it down into scores of products, systems, and trainings that I've performed for thousands of businesses and marketing agencies around the world.

With today's technology, businesses have more power, more speed, more information, and more clout than ever before. Sadly, most don't realize it, but I am changing that. My primary goal is to help businesses recover $100 million dollars in lost sales. My secondary goal is to train people in need of work, such as corporate-castoffs (like me), military veterans, or mothers returning to the workplace, the skills to help the businesses in their community snatch the low-hanging fruit that so many of them miss every day.

I'm pleased to say that we are off to an exceptional start! We convert prospects into paying customers, customers into repeat customers, and repeat customers into champions of the business who will refer it to their family and friends. It's a great system that leads to higher sales, higher profits, and much happier sales staff and business owners.

My name is Steve Rosenbaum. I put businesses in front of prospects at the right time, at the right place, with the right message, and in the right market so they make more sales.

ABOUT THE AUTHOR

Steve Rosenbaum, is an entrepreneur, author, business advisor, product developer, and leader that inspires and mentors tens of thousands businesses and professionals worldwide to get more sales and improve their bottom line.

Regarded as "The Original" Back End Specialist, Steve founded ZapPowee and created the first Back End Specialist Certification program with the core mission of teaching others his skills so that they could help local businesses in their area survive and thrive; a true "Win-Win" that addresses two of the biggest problems facing our economy today.

Steve has a special gift, just for "So What Do You Do" readers! Claim your free gift at zaplink.us/swdyd

facebook.com/steverosenbaum

ABOUT THE AUTHOR

Joel Comm

Joel Comm is a New York Times Best-Selling author, Internationally-known speaker and Internet pioneer. Online since 1995, Joel has inspired, equipped and entertained millions of people through his websites, software products, books, training and broadcasts. His previous titled include: *The AdSense Code: What Google Never Told You About Making Money with AdSense, Click Here to Order: Stories of the World's Most Successful Internet Marketing Entrepreneurs, Twitter Power: How to Dominate Your Market One Tweet at a Time* and *KaChing: How to Run an Online Business that Pays and Pays.*

FREE MEMBERSHIP!

Claim Your Free Membership, Bonuses and an Opportunity to Be Featured in a Future Volume of "So What Do YOU Do?", for book buyers only!

Joel Comm and the So What Do You Do Authors would like to present you free access to a number of free bonuses which are yours for the asking. As a book buyer, you are eligible to receive free reports, audios, videos and memberships related to the expertise of a number of the authors within.

Would you like your story to appear in a future volume of So What Do You Do? If you are an expert in your field, you may apply to be considered for a chapter! To claim your bonuses and find an application to be included in a future volume, go to:

SoWhatDoYouDo.com